tried by fire
the message of 1 peter

tried by fire

the message of 1 peter

william c. brownson

baker book house
grand rapids, michigan

Scripture passages from **The New English Bible,** © The Delegates of the Oxford University Press, and the Syndics of the Cambridge University Press 1961, 1970, are used with permission of Oxford University Press. Texts quoted from the **Revised Standard Version of the Bible,** copyrighted 1946 and 1952 by the Division of Christian Education, National Council of the Churches of Christ in America are used by permission. Those from **The New Testament in Modern English** translated by J. B. Phillips © 1960 are used by permission of the Macmillan Company, New York.

This material originally appeared as a series of articles in *The Church Herald*, the weekly organ of the Reformed Church in America.

Printed in the United States of America

contents

Chapter One

is there any hope?

*Blessed be the God and Father of our Lord Jesus
Christ! By his great mercy we have been born anew
to a living hope through the resurrection of Jesus
Christ from the dead, and to an inheritance which
is imperishable, undefiled, and unfading, kept in
heaven for you, who by God's power are guarded
through faith for a salvation ready to be revealed in
the last time* (I Peter 1:3-5, RSV).

A thousand grim voices herald the death of hope. Witness
the writings of Camus and Kafka, in which the future is
always bleak and forbidding. Or turn to the "theatre of the
absurd." The language breakdown in *Waiting for Godot* por-
trays the collapse of meaningful existence for modern man.
Artists like Francis Bacon of England splash horror and
desperation on every canvas. Each of these proclaims boldly
what millions secretly suspect—that man "come of age" has
nothing left to hope for.

How sharp the contrast to the mood with which we began
this century! We were hopeful then. We dreamed that man
was innately good and that progress was inevitable. We saw
mankind moving forward and upward, "working out the
beast and letting ape and tiger die." But that seems so long
ago. Now we are wiser and sadder. We have seen what
happened at Dachau and Auschwitz, at Pearl Harbor and
Hiroshima. We've watched with horror the arms race and the
arming of the races. We've heard the shots in Dallas, in
Memphis, in Los Angeles. Our dreams have been smashed and

7

a dark cynicism has stolen upon us. The hope that flourished in the optimism of the nineteenth century lies dead.

But not all hopes die. Peter the apostle wrote to the Christians in his time about a "living hope." Here were people who gloried not in what man could become, but in what God had done. He had raised Jesus Christ from the dead. By that resurrection His followers had become new people. As new people they found life suffused with a new hope—a hope that could not die, because the one in whom they hoped had conquered death.

For what did they hope? To what did they look forward? "To an inheritance," writes Peter. That would have a familiar ring for Jewish readers. They had heard much of the inheritance which God held in store for His people. The Holy Land was their portion. God had promised it to them when they were wanderers in the earth and freed them for it when they were slaves. He had led them to it through a howling wilderness. He had brought them back to it from bondage and exile.

But even the land flowing with milk and honey did not fulfill Israel's hopes. The land of their longings was often polluted by idolatry, torn by the strife of brethren, and overrun by invaders. Could this be the inheritance? Was there nothing more than this to hope for?

We Americans know how they felt. We cherished great dreams about our land, too. To us it was another Canaan, a new beginning, the "last best hope of earth." Our natural resources and technological know-how have made it a fairyland of abundance. We have become the most powerful and envied nation on earth. But all this beauty hides an ugliness, and all this radiant health a plague—as the events of our time have made all too plain. Those who have found "a place in the sun" are bored with it; those who struggle for what has been denied them are often disillusioned when the prize is grasped. Surely there must be something more to yearn for than this!

Canaans, past or present, do not constitute the living hope. The inheritance for which Christians look is "imperishable, undefiled, and unfading." It is not reached by wilderness wanderings or ocean journeys. It is "kept in heaven." Otherworldly? Yes, decidedly. Heavenly? Unashamedly so. This is a treasure laid up where, in Jesus' words, "neither moth nor rust consumes, and where thieves do not break in and steal."

But isn't this the same old pie-in-the-sky bit? Isn't this the drug that the ruling classes have always used to keep the enslaved and deprived content with their lot? Doesn't this kind of star-gazing turn our attention away from the urgent problems that cry out for solution in today's world? Obviously, the answer to these questions is that the Christian hope, like every other good thing, can be misunderstood and abused. But didn't those early Christians, for whom the living hope was so bright and vibrant, prove to be the salt of this earth and the light of this world? Peter himself, in this same letter, had many wise and urgent things to say about life in the here-and-now. Still, he exulted in the "living hope."

The issue is not the always sterile choice, "Shall we focus on this world or the next?" The deeper question is, "Does the future belong to man's pride, or to God's grace?" In Jesus Christ, God has triumphed over every evil power, over all despair, over death itself. The "new heaven and the new earth," however we may serve its coming, is not our achievement, but the Father's gift. And this inheritance, this hope, is sure!

Yes, but how sure is it for you—one among three billion, in this last third of the twentieth century? Who are the heirs that are certain to receive it? Peter answers, those "who by God's power are guarded." Christians are even now being sustained by God's hand for the salvation yet to be revealed. But that keeping power is not a force from without, not a mechanical constraint. They are "guarded through faith." Do you want to be sure of God's inheritance? Then fix your attention in faith on the risen Lord. See in Him the might and mercy of our heavenly Father. Commit yourself in trust to His rule. And as you trust, He will keep you.

There is hope for the hopeless. The future is as bright as the first Easter morning. No wonder Peter began with a call to praise: "Blessed be the God and Father of our Lord Jesus Christ!"

Chapter Two

astounding joy

This is cause for great joy, even though now you smart for a little while, if need be, under trials of many kinds. Even gold passes through the assayer's fire, and more precious than perishable gold is faith which has stood the test. These trials come so that your faith may prove itself worthy of all praise, glory, and honour when Christ is revealed. You have not seen him, yet you love him; and trusting in him now without seeing him, you are transported with a joy too great for words, while you reap the harvest of your faith, that is salvation for your souls (I Peter 1:6-9, NEB).

Most of us have had our moments of stunning gladness. Perhaps they burst on us in the words of a doctor, "It's a boy! Mother and son are doing fine." Or, after anxious pacing outside an operating room, "The tumor is benign." Perhaps in your case it was the first thrilling awareness that the love of your life really cared for you. Or when you welcomed back your boy—safe and sound—from the front lines.

But those were high moments. In the course of a lifetime we have very few like that. And most people think of joy, don't they, as spasmodic, occasional, confined to never-to-be-forgotten crises?

Peter writes about a joy with staying power. He has told of the living hope we have through Christ. Now he points to the rejoicing which it brings. Here is joy that doesn't wait for a sudden turn of circumstances. In fact, it persists even when the conditions of life are anything but cheering. The believers whom Peter addresses, for example, were smarting "under trials of many kinds." There was the ridicule and scorn of those who despised the new faith. The powers that be had hounded or harassed them from time to time for their allegiance to Christ as Lord. And then there were the common struggles and sorrows which they shared with those about them. For children are not always healthy at birth. Nor are tumors always benign. Love is sometimes not requited, and some yearned-for faces never return from the wars. Yet, amid stresses like these, Christians could greatly rejoice.

Their faith gave them reasons for gladness—"cause for great joy." For one thing, the trials were "for a little while." How much depends on our perspective! If this life is all there is, then any time of affliction seems long, unbearably long. But those who have known eternal life already breaking in on them in Christ can see life's struggles against a vast background. For them these things are "but for a moment." They will not last; they have no final power over us.

What is more, sufferings serve to "prove" our faith. Some see in life's hardships only the cruelty of other men or the quirks of a blind fate. Christians see them as the "assayer's fire." In the midst of them faith is refined and purified. Faith that has been in the crucible will shine with a goldlike luster when Christ comes.

What, after all, is genuine in our protestations of faith? Believers who are very warm and very articulate can also be very shallow. It is easy to be orthodox, easy to speak with ringing conviction when the sea of life is relatively calm. But let the storms come; let bitter, desolating hours overtake us: they will do for us what sunny skies and smiling circumstances never could. You can rejoice, says Peter, in the blackest and worst of your days. Just then, God is making something of your life that will honor Him at His appearing.

But these reasonings of faith, however cogent and compelling, do not always produce joy. We can be told that our anguish will not last and that the furnace of affliction is making purer gold of us, and still know little gladness in it all.

What Christian—even the gloomiest—hasn't heard all that many times before? Christianity offers a cheering doctrine, indeed; but it offers much more. This blend of suffering and joy, this new thing that broke upon an incredulous world in the first century, had more behind it than a new theology. Even with the best rationale for rejoicing, men need a gladdening power to bear them through. And this dynamic the early Christians found in a personal relationship to the living Christ.

Hear how Peter puts it: "You have not seen him, yet you love him . . . ." What a strange combination of words! The relationship of which they lyrically sing is unique. What? Can you love someone deeply, devotedly, without ever having seen him? Yes, Christians do love Christ, love Him just so. Napoleon marveled at this and expressed the wonder of it well: "An extraordinary power of influencing and commanding men has been given to Alexander, Charlemagne, and myself. But with us the presence has been necessary, the eye, the voice, the hand. Whereas Jesus Christ has influenced and commanded his subjects without his bodily presence for eighteen hundred years."

But how does this love for an unseen Christ arise in a human heart? Peter continues: "trusting in him now without seeing him." Love springs from faith. We love Christ because we are persuaded that He first loved us. But again the paradox: we believe in Him without seeing Him. A superficial naturalism says, "Seeing is believing." Christian faith turns it around and proclaims that believing is seeing.

> Lord, thou hast made thyself to me
> A living, bright reality;
> More present to faith's vision keen
> Than any earthly object seen.

Here is how a personal relationship to Jesus Christ is established. We learn of Him in the preaching of the gospel and in the witness of Scripture. By the power of the Holy Spirit we respond in faith, and Christ becomes real to us as our living Lord and Savior. Trusting then in Him, we love

Him and seek to please Him. And in this relationship of personal trust and love, says Peter, we are "transported with a joy too great for words." We rejoice *in Christ*, in the crucified and risen one who has become our very life. Yes, Christians still do, even in suffering. Pastor Niemöller in his last sermon on June 27, 1937, shortly before being imprisoned proclaimed boldly: "There is indeed no hope except to hold firm to the crucified one and learn to say in simple and therefore certain faith, 'In the bottom of my heart thy name and cross alone shine forth at all times and in all hours *and therefore I can be glad.*' "

This is the astounding joy. This is the sign that the salvation yet to come is becoming ours already. Suffering and sadness are not the last things about the world. They are next to last. The last best thing is "the laughter deep in the hearts of the saints." Christ has said it and they have found it true: "Lo, I am with you all the days."

Chapter Three

what good is the old testament?

> *The prophets who prophesied of the grace that was
> to be yours searched and inquired about this salva-
> tion; they inquired what person or time was indi-
> cated by the Spirit of Christ within them when
> predicting the sufferings of Christ and the sub-
> sequent glory. It was revealed to them that they
> were serving not themselves but you, in the things
> which have now been announced to you by those
> who preached the good news to you through the
> Holy Spirit sent from heaven, things into which
> angels long to look* (I Peter 1:10-12, RSV).

What good is the Old Testament? Have you ever wondered
about that? Many Christians have. In the early history of the
church an influential Christian named Marcion insisted that
Christians should reject the Old Testament. Marcion claimed
that the God of the Old Testament was a God of wrath,
completely different from the God of love whom Jesus
revealed in the New. This point of view was never accepted
by most Christians, but the problem which it raises is still
with us. Many in the church today see little value in Old
Testament Scripture. "That collection of laws, those endless
sacrifices, those obscure prophecies—what do they all mean
to us?"

The apostle Peter can help us significantly—right at this
point. He has something to say about what the Old Testament meant for him and for the early Christians to whom he

wrote. Perhaps his message can make the Old Testament come alive for you as it has for others.

Peter tells us first what the Old Testament is all about. What is this collection of thirty-nine books, written by so many different authors, over such a long period of time? Is there one unifying motif, one central theme that runs through the whole? Yes, there is. Peter says that the Old Testament writers wrote about "this salvation," the living hope in which Christians have such joy. The Old Testament, together with the New, is a book of salvation. Its theme is the saving purpose of God; its history is the record of how that purpose has been unfolding.

More specifically, the Old Testament speaks of "the sufferings of Christ and the subsequent glory." It points toward the one who is the central figure of the New Testament, Jesus Christ our Lord. But you say, "I don't see this connection. I can't find much about Christ in the Old Testament." Neither could Peter, even for years after he knew Jesus. But there came a time after the resurrection of Christ when the apostles received the most significant course in Biblical interpretation that was ever given. The instruction began on the Emmaus road when Jesus spoke to the two travelers with whom He walked. "O foolish men and slow of heart to believe all that the prophets have spoken! Was it not necessary that the Christ should suffer these things and enter into his glory? And beginning with Moses and all the prophets he interpreted to them in all the Scriptures the things concerning himself" (Luke 24:25-27). Then, on that same Easter evening, before the gathered disciples in Jerusalem He said, "These are my words which I spoke to you while I was still with you, that everything written about me in the law of Moses and the prophets and the psalms must be fulfilled. Then he opened their minds to understand the Scriptures." By the teaching of the Lord Himself and by the illumination of the Holy Spirit, the early Christians found that Old Testament Scripture spoke of their risen Savior and of the grace which had come to them in Him. They studied the Old Testament in that light—and so should we.

This did not mean, however, that the whole message of the

Christian gospel had been clearly told in the Old Testament. As Peter points out, the prophets themselves did not fully grasp the meaning of these things. They "searched and inquired about this salvation." They sought with great eagerness to understand how the saving purpose of God would be realized in this world. They were not sure "what person or time was indicated by the Spirit of Christ within them." In fact, it was revealed to them that the things of which they spoke had meaning beyond their own generation, a meaning which they could but dimly discern.

Here we touch on an issue that is crucial for the understanding of prophecy. Interpreters have often clustered at two extremes. One group tends to see in the writings of the prophets only the prediction of future events, as though the prophet had nothing to say to his own time. The other group, in reaction against this emphasis, majors in the prophet's message to his own generation. But we cannot do justice to the writings of the prophets, especially as seen in the light of the New Testament, unless we combine these two perspectives. The prophet did have a message for his own generation, and any sound interpretation of prophecy must begin there—finding the original meaning in the setting out of which the prophecy arose. But we cannot stop with that. There is also a forward look. In all that the prophets said about the fulfillment of God's salvation, God was speaking through them of things which only future generations could fully appreciate.

So relevant is the message of the Old Testament for us that Peter can write to his Christian friends that "they [the prophets] were serving not themselves but you." They wrote for their contemporaries, yes, but they wrote also for us, and the things they wrote for us bear directly on the gospel which is now being preached throughout the whole world. The Old Testament sheds its light on the present-day proclamation of Jesus Christ. Only against its background of creation, calling, and covenant can the good news of Jesus Christ be rightly understood and appreciated. The whole Bible is the Spirit inspired witness both of prophets and apostles to God's saving design in Jesus Christ our Lord.

And these things, continues Peter, are "things into which

angels long to look." What can he mean by this? We learn elsewhere in Scripture that there is rejoicing among the angels in heaven over one sinner who repents. It is not surprising, then, that the message of joy and salvation of which Scripture speaks should excite the awe and interest of heavenly beings.

Ponder for a moment what all this means. If the prophets prophesied for us, and the apostles preached for us, and if their message calls forth even the fascination of the angels, we ought to look into these things, too. With reverent eagerness then, praying for the Spirit's guidance, let us *search the Scriptures*—the Old Testament as well as the New!

Chapter Four

the best of both worlds

> *Therefore gird up your minds, be sober, set your*
> *hope fully upon the grace that is coming to you at*
> *the revelation of Jesus Christ. As obedient chil-*
> *dren, do not be conformed to the passions of your*
> *former ignorance, but as he who called you is holy,*
> *be holy yourselves in all your conduct; since it is*
> *written, "You shall be holy, for I am holy"* (I Peter
> 1:13-16, RSV).

Tongue in cheek, *Time* quipped recently that a certain political aspirant was "promising the best of both worlds." That calls forth a wry smile from most of us. We have come to suspect the rosy dream that we can, at one and the same time, lower the national debt and reduce taxes. We seriously doubt that if each man does as he pleases now, it will work out best for everyone in the end. We are inclined to think that a man has to choose his "world." Must not Christians, at least, choose between this world and the next, between the here and now and the there and then? If you really want the blessings of heaven, so runs the argument, you have to forget about the affairs of earth, or vice versa.

But the apostle Peter did not see it that way. Nor, for that matter, did any of the New Testament writers. They had a remarkable concern about both worlds. Peter, for example, has a twofold challenge for his Christian friends in this brief paragraph. He calls them to *hope* and to *be holy*.

On the one hand, the apostle expects Christians to be totally oriented toward the future. After a passage on the wonders of God's mercy in Christ comes this charge: "Set your hope fully upon the grace that is coming to you at the revelation of Jesus Christ." Disciples are to look forward eagerly to the day when Christ's glory will be fully revealed, and to the mercy and full salvation which will then be theirs. In a sense this grace is "coming" to them even now—it's on the way. They have had a taste of it already. And yet they are to rest the full weight of their hopes on what is yet to be.

Does it sound strange—being exhorted to hope like this? Who urges people today to set their hopes on Christ's appearing? But see how Peter calls for concentrated effort in this direction. "Gird up your minds," he says. He is talking about a preparation for action. Flowing robes might give an air of dignity to a Greek philosopher or a Roman official, but they were hardly the garb for a strenuous contest. "Brace yourself! Get set!" he seems to say. "Hope with all your might for his appearing." And this requires not only girding for action but also alertness. "Be sober," says Peter, or, as Phillips translates it, be "as men who know what they are doing." Don't let anything deaden or distract you. Keep yourself in full possession of all your faculties so that nothing dims your anticipation.

Does this make sense for today? Why should we call people in the United States to embrace this hope when they have it so good right here? Perhaps that is part of our problem. You sense in Peter's urgent writing the overhanging threat of persecution, the felt uncertainty of life in this world, the poverty in which most Christians lived. Why shouldn't they hope? But you sense more than that. You sense also that the Christ whom they love without having seen (1:8) is unspeakably real and precious to them. That is why the prospect of His coming can be such an object of longing and hope. To love Him is to "love his appearing."

But what keeps this hope in Christ's return from becoming an unhealthy flight from reality? Peter hastens to add that the future hope is not the only dimension of Christian living.

We are to hope "as children of obedience"—as those whose very nature it is to obey. We are to live as though obedience to the Father were our outstanding family trait.

The apostle now spells out in a fuller way what he means by a life of obedience. First, on the negative side, "Do not be conformed to the passions of your former ignorance." Once they did not know God. Once they willfully suppressed what knowledge of Him they did have. Then their lives were ruled by their own desires, driven this way and that by conflicting passions. Now the will of God is to be the focus and aim of their conduct. They must no longer be conformed (remember Rom. 12:2?) to the old pattern. The old way meant embracing the standards and values of the society around them. Someone has put the recipe for the life of disobedience like this: "Find out what they're thinking and think it; find out what they're doing and do it; find out what they're wanting and want it."

Peter urges that the life of the Christian be fashioned in a better mold. "As he who called you is holy, be holy yourselves in all your conduct." Quite a different pattern! Here it is not the mores of the prevailing culture but the revealed character of God which becomes the Christian's model. God's "holiness" is in a real sense his "Godness." The term gathers together all that He has revealed of Himself as the sovereign, gracious creator and redeemer. For us, to be holy means to be set apart for this God and for His purposes in the world. It means belonging especially to Him, becoming more and more like Him, dealing with the world around us as He has dealt with us in Christ. "You shall be holy for I am holy." This is His command and also His promise. By the power of His Holy Spirit He is working in our lives to conform us to the image of Christ. We, in turn, are to make that likeness to the Savior the end of all our striving. Is He the seeker of lost sheep? Then so must we be shepherds. Is He the faithful witness to the truth of God? We must bear our testimony, too. Does He spend Himself that men may have life and have it abundantly? Then so must we, in His name. His servant ministry is to be ours as well.

Do you notice how Peter holds "worldly" and "otherworldly"—obedience in this world and hope for the next—very closely together? These are not meant to be enemies or alternatives but allies. In wholesome Christian experience they enrich and sustain each other. Christians are called here and now to hope and holiness—the best of both worlds.

Chapter Five

living in fear

If you pray to a Father who judges men by their
actions without the slightest favoritism, then you
should spend the time of your stay here on earth
with reverent fear. For you must realize all the
time that you have been "ransomed" from the
futile way of living passed on to you by your
fathers' traditions, not with some money payment
of transient value, but by the costly shedding of
blood. The price was in fact the lifeblood of Christ,
the unblemished and unstained lamb of sacrifice. It
is true that God chose him to fulfill his part before
the world was founded, but it was for your benefit
that he was revealed in these last days—for you
who found your faith in God through Christ. And
God raised him from the dead and gave him un-
imaginable splendor, so that all your faith and
hope might be centered in God (I Peter 1:17-21,
Phillips).

Fear haunts our streets. One-third of all Americans, says a
recent news magazine, are afraid to walk in their own neigh-
borhoods after dark. No wonder "law and order" becomes
such an emotionally charged issue in every political cam-
paign! None of us wants to live in the shadow of fear.

How strange then that the Christian faith should recommend that we "spend the time of our stay here on earth in
fear." Surely this can't be meant for us! Most Americans look

on freedom from fear as one of our "inalienable rights." Yet here it is in Holy Scripture—the insistent call that Christians live in fear. What can we make of this?

Peter gives two reasons for his summons to fearfulness. First, *the God whom we call "Father" is an impartial judge.* The apostle seems to be alluding here to the opening words of the Lord's Prayer. Apparently from the beginnings of the Christian church, disciples were accustomed to pray the prayer which their Lord had taught them. They had learned from Him that God wills to be known as a gracious Father to His people. But "Father" on Jesus' lips never meant a sentimental, indulgent pushover. Peter reminds his readers of that fact. This Father is the one to whom we must answer for what we have done with our lives.

Christians suffer from considerable confusion about this matter of judgment. There is a sense in which the Judgment Day for believers is past already. Those who trust in Christ will never be condemned, for He was condemned in their stead. They can exult with the apostle Paul, "There is therefore now no condemnation to them which are in Christ Jesus." But that is not the end of the New Testament message on judgment. Though no believer will ever be banished from God's presence, yet all must give account of themselves to Him. "We must all appear before the judgment seat of Christ," says the apostle Paul, "so that each one may receive good or evil according to what he has done in the body." Make no mistake of-it, warns the apostle, there is a reckoning which makes a difference.

Our Lord's teaching also is clear and insistent on this point. We have a stewardship to answer for. We have an account to give. Think of it—all of life passing under His review! Daniel Webster was not exaggerating when he said, "The most important thought I ever had was that of my individual responsibility to God."

A real apprehension of what God's judgment means shatters all presumption. The Judge of all the earth winks at nothing. With Him there are no special allowances for privileged people, nor can He be put off by fair sounding excuses. Before Him at last, the secrets of the heart are secrets no longer and we will be seen for what we really are. Can we be trivial now when *that* lies ahead of us? "Spend the time of your stay here on earth with reverent fear."

But the apostle has another reason—an even more compelling one: *We were redeemed at great cost.* Christians have been rescued from a "futile way of living." Many to whom Peter was writing had inherited an empty way of life from godless parents; their lives in turn had been meaningless and vain. But now Christ has ransomed them, and Peter reminds them who their great redeemer is. He was a Savior chosen by God "before the world was founded." Now He has been revealed in history "for your benefit," says Peter. For it is through Christ that they have come to know and trust in God. This same Jesus has been raised from the dead and given "unimaginable splendor," so that all their trust may be in the gracious One who has exalted Him.

Why this interlude on the glory and greatness of Christ? Because Peter wants them to realize what redemption really means. He longs that they may glimpse the surpassing wonder of what has been done for them. You must realize, he urges, that you were ransomed "not with some money payment of transient value but by the costly shedding of blood." It was a redemption through *death*. That must always give it weight and solemnity. But more, it was by the lifeblood of Christ, "the unblemished and unstained lamb of sacrifice." The word "Christ" is in an emphatic position. Here is the marvel and grandeur of it all: the life poured out for men was the life of *Christ*. Live in reverent fear, says the apostle, when you remember this.

It becomes evident, doesn't it, that Peter is speaking of a special kind of fear. He wants no numbing terror, no servile cowering, no dread of God that makes us hide or run from Him. Call it *awe* if you will. Call it a vivid awareness that He is real—the God of judgment and grace. Call it a style of life—remembering our accountability to Him and treasuring His costly love for us. This is "the fear of the Lord." Strange to say, for many it is the key to courage and to peace. When we fear God, nothing else need cause us fear.

Chapter Six

born again-for what?

> *Having purified your souls by your obedience to the truth for a sincere love of the brethren, love one another earnestly from the heart. You have been born anew, not of perishable seed but of imperishable, through the living and abiding word of God; for "All flesh is like grass and all its glory like the flower of grass. The grass withers, and the flower falls, but the word of the Lord abides forever"* (I Peter 1:22-25, RSV).

"Born again." What does that phrase mean to you? For some, the words are pure gold. They stand for all that is vital in the Christian faith. They are the touchstone of its authenticity. They spell the difference between a hollow, outward profession on the one hand, and a warm, transforming Christian experience on the other. From this standpoint, to describe someone as a "real born-again Christian" is to place on him the stamp of highest approval.

Have you heard that description? Most often it is used of those who can testify to a definite, life-changing encounter with Jesus Christ. Often the reality of the new birth is seen as so central and so significant that this initial experience of God's grace is spoken of in glowing terms for many years after it has occurred.

There are others in our churches, however, who are uneasy with the phrase "born again." These also name the name of

Christ, but in most instances cannot recall a distinct, dramatic crossroad in life where they first met Him. They feel somewhat uncomfortable—perhaps even a trifle envious—when they hear others speak enthusiastically of the new birth. But more than that, believers in this latter group frankly doubt the value of the whole emphasis. They are suspicious of a style of life in which Christians are continually harking back to what happened long ago. They fear that sometimes "experience" may be regarded more highly than discipleship. "Being born again" may be all well and good, they acknowledge; but the important thing is "being Christian" here and now.

Maybe these points of view are not so new. Perhaps there is a tension here which has a long history. At any rate, what Peter had to say in this ancient letter seems admirably suited to both groups. However we feel about the new birth, we can learn something from him.

To begin with, for Peter the new life is a fact—a fact for all Christians. "You have been born anew," he writes to his scattered brethren. How did that happen? Peter answers, "through the living and abiding word of God." God's Word is like a seed, yet not a fragile thing, blown by the wind, subject itself to decay. No, this is the never fading, undying Word of the living God. And how was it planted in their lives, that it might quicken them to new life? By the preaching of "the good news." Peter here seems to be putting in his own words the parable he heard from the lips of his Master. The good seed is the Word of God and the sower is the one who proclaims it. That seed, wherever men truly receive it, brings forth life and fruit.

"But what is this Word of God?" asks someone. Some say it is the living Word, Christ. Others contend that it is the written Word of Scripture. Which is it? Peter answers that it is *both*—and the preached Word, too. It is Christ Himself, of course, who gives life to men by His Spirit. But He does so not in a vacuum, but through the witness of prophets and apostles, recorded in Holy Scripture. And that Word, revealed in history and in Scripture, speaks to us afresh through those who preach and teach the gospel today.

But Peter's main concern here is not to tell how the new birth has come about, and certainly not to describe how it feels to be born again. His immediate interest is the practical issue. What happens as a result?

Peter reminds them that they have "purified their souls by their obedience to the truth." That is, the same Word which makes us alive also cleanses us. Remember the familiar words of the psalmist? "How can a young man keep his way pure? By guarding it according to thy word. . . . I have laid up thy word in my heart that I might not sin against thee" (Ps. 119:9, 11). Notice that this involves some action on the part of those who hear. The Word does not work on us automatically. We experience the power of the truth when we *obey* it. An interesting phrase, that one—"obedience to the truth." The New Testament writers seem to use faith and obedience almost interchangeably. As Dietrich Bonhoeffer crisply put it, "Only he who believes obeys; only he who obeys believes."

Now we come to the central emphasis of the entire passage. What is the new birth for? What does this inner cleansing produce? According to Peter, the goal is "a sincere love of the brethren." Two things about it call for notice. Though it reaches out to all those around us, it is first of all a love for our fellow Christians. Just as those in our immediate family have a particular claim on our love, so we have a special responsibility for brothers and sisters in Christ. And let it be, says Peter, "sincere" love. Few people are fooled—or helped—by a show of affection which is not deeply meant.

All right, says Peter, here is what new life and cleansing are meant for. You Christians have a new freedom, a new capacity to love each other. Now you see that you do it! Love each other from the heart. Love earnestly—with an energetic, active kind of love. Love, he seems to remind them, is something you *do*.

Well, what about this "born again" idea, in the light of Peter's words? If we tend to be skittish about the term, let's listen again. To our Lord and His apostles, the new birth was a momentous reality. On the other hand, if we are fond of the idea, if we treasure the experience, let's remember where the new birth should lead us and get down to the business of loving our brothers. And why not try starting with those who don't quite see it our way?

Chapter Seven

growing up

*So put away all malice and all guile and insincerity
and envy and all slander. Like newborn babes, long
for the pure spiritual milk, that by it you may
grow up to salvation; for you have tasted the
kindness of the Lord* (I Peter 2:1-3, RSV).

Where there's life, there's growth. A bit of new wood, a
batch of fresh cells, perhaps a tiny green shoot—every living
thing is growing somehow. That's the way life is. Whatever
stops growing is on its way out.

The same holds true for new life, the life which Christ
gives. It can never stand still or mark time. Growth is its
fundamental law. To be alive in Jesus Christ is to be on your
way toward maturity. And that means growth.

When you are young, when life is surging most strongly in
you, you want to grow. What third grade boy, watching
wide-eyed while the mighty varsity plays, doesn't long for the
day when he too will be a man? At least, that's the way it is
at our house. Our four boys aspire to be basketball players.
For that, you need height. We have so many recorded mea-
surements on our family growth chart that the pencil marks
almost all run together. After all, how much taller can anyone get in a week's time!

Vital Christians want to grow, too. It is to that life force in
them that Peter is appealing here. Christian, you have been
made alive in Jesus Christ, quickened through the Word of
the gospel. But that's only the beginning. There's nothing

cute about prolonged infancy. God wants you to "grow up to salvation." He wants you to move toward the wholeness of a life that is genuinely Christlike. And Peter is writing to show the way.

First, there is a negative side to this growing business. "So put away all malice and all guile and insincerity and envy and all slander." There are some things, apparently, that can really stunt our growth. Peter names a few of them right here. The purpose of the new birth, he has already told us, is to lead us to genuine, open-hearted love. No claims to spiritual life can stand up if we fail to manifest authentic Christian caring. Quite evidently, these ugly traits that Peter now mentions are serious obstacles on the way toward love.

"Malice" is a kind of settled ill will, a downright meanness of disposition. "Guile" and "insincerity" describe the basic phoniness which may pretend to be sweet and friendly but is actually quite the opposite. This sort of "love" may pat you on the back, but you never know when the hand has a knife in it. And then there is "envy." What could be more loveless than that—actually feeling bad about another's good fortune, —getting bitter and nasty when someone else is honored? Envy leads naturally into "slander"—running down, belittling, disparaging someone else's character.

All growth toward fullness of life in Christ is seriously impeded if we harbor attitudes and qualities like these. Put them away decisively, says Peter. Strip them off as you would a soiled and foul smelling garment. Shun them as you would some plague that threatened your life.

But don't stop there. Renouncing evil is not the only requisite for growth, any more than germ-free conditions are all a baby needs. Antiseptics are a great boon, but you can't grow on them. For growth you need food, and as a Christian the food you require is "the pure spiritual milk."

The Greek word translated "spiritual," *logikon*, is a near cousin to the Greek *logos*, which means "word." Peter means a spiritual milk as contrasted to the natural liquid; but he is also carrying on further what he had said earlier about the "living, abiding word of God." The nourishment on which Christians feed is the gospel, the message of God's grace in

Jesus Christ. They have been born anew through that Word and cleansed by it, but that is not the end. The very gospel which has quickened them to life becomes now the means of their sustenance and growth. The Christ who gives us life is the Christ by whom we live and grow. All progress toward Christian maturity comes through appropriating more fully the Savior who comes to us in the gospel. It is a process of coming to know Christ better, of being more wholly conformed to His image. It means a deepened learning of Him as He meets us in the pages of Scripture and in the witness of our fellow Christians.

Since that is true, every Christian is to "long for" the spiritual milk. Yes, crave it, says Peter, "as newborn babes." What a vivid picture that is! Have you ever watched a baby when feeding time comes? Let him once touch his bottle or his mother's breast and he's a pink flurry of feverish excitement. Arms and legs thrash out in all directions. He squirms and sputters and struggles until at last he gets a taste of the life-giving liquid. Then he's content—at least until you try to take it away!

But isn't that a bit exaggerated? A vivid figure of speech perhaps, but isn't it a little too much to expect? Does anybody ever crave the Word of God like that? Yes, some have. There were days in England when copies of Scripture were so scarce, and thirst for the living water so great, that Bibles had to be fastened with chains in the churches. Today many of us have several copies of Scripture in our homes, and they hardly need to be chained! But if we want to grow as Christians, it is time to dust them off and study them. Just how keen is your appetite? That can be a searching personal question—maybe an index of your Christian health. What about setting up a regular daily schedule for Bible study? Most people find it helpful to plan their *eating* that way. The discipline may even stimulate your appetite.

Peter has one more grand incentive for the study of God's Word: "For you have tasted the kindness of the Lord." You know how it is with snacks. Once you get a taste of something you really like, it tastes like *more*. Someone made plenty on the potato chips slogan, "Can't stop eatin' 'em."

This holds true for many types of food, as frustrated weight-watchers ruefully admit.

And that homely fact of life suggests a far higher truth; namely, the more we know of Christ the more we want to know. You Christians, says Peter, have tasted and seen that the Lord is good. You know what He means to you. You know the difference that He has made in your life. You have caught a glimpse of His marvelous kindness. You have begun to know the power of His transforming friendship. Well then, keep on learning of Him. Feed on His Word, that you may grow in His likeness!

Chapter Eight

that living stone

Come to him, to that living stone, rejected by men but in God's sight chosen and precious; and like living stones be yourselves built into a spiritual house, to be a holy priesthood, to offer spiritual sacrifices acceptable to God through Jesus Christ. For it stands in scripture: "Behold, I am laying in Zion a stone, a cornerstone chosen and precious, and he who believes in him will not be put to shame." To you therefore who believe, he is precious, but for those who do not believe, "The very stone which the builders rejected has become the head of the corner," and "A stone that will make men stumble, a rock that will make them fall"; for they stumble because they disobey the word, as they were destined to do (I Peter 2:4-8, RSV).

It was a bold, jarring way to speak of his Lord—"that living stone." Peter would hardly have spoken so had not Jesus already applied the term to Himself: "The very stone which the builders rejected has become the head of the corner." Not just any stone lying in a field, or a slab of rock in a quarry—the Greek word means a "worked" stone, a stone fitted for building, ready to be used. But, of all things, a *living* stone! Christ is the foundation, the cornerstone on which the church rests, but He is more than that. He is the risen one, alive Himself, and able to enter into vital personal fellowship with His people.

Christ claimed all that for Himself, didn't He? He told men that to heed His word was to build on the only solid foundation. To all who were searching for what it means to live He offered Himself as "the life" and the life giver. But some would have nothing to do with Him. Religious leaders and government authorities joined hands to destroy Him. He was "despised and rejected by men." But how different were God's thoughts! In His sight the rejected one, the crucified one, was "chosen and precious." He was God's elect, God's well-beloved, God's Son.

In fact, God raised Him from the dead. Now He, the living stone, stands in the path of Everyman. Wherever His Word is preached, men are confronted by Him. They may scorn and reject Him, but their rejection does not end the matter. He becomes to them then "a stone that will make men stumble, a rock that will make them fall."

Why do they stumble? Why are some broken on this Rock rather than built on it?. "Because they disobey the word," Peter answers. Or, as the New English Bible translates it, "They disbelieve the Word." Both translations are correct. Unbelief and disobedience are two sides of the same coin. When men hear the good news, Christ stands before them as their rightful Lord. Either they trust Him and submit to His rule, or they show themselves unbelieving and disobedient. But they are not the same. No man can hear Christ's call and remain the same. Christ is the searching light that shines into our darkness. When we glimpse that light, we either come to it to be revealed for what we are, or like frightened haters of light we scurry farther into the shadows. We never stay where we are. No wonder Jesus said so solemnly, "Take heed how you hear."

Now comes that strange, mysterious word: "They stumble . . . as they were destined to do." What, then—had they never a chance? Were they doomed beforehand to this rejection? Are they simply acting out an inexorable divine decree? No. To put it that way is to distort and falsify the Biblical message. God's purpose is never static, never cut-and-dried, never grim and mechanical. Men are not pawns or puppets, manipulated in a cosmic scheme. They are responsible—

awesomely responsible—for what they do with God's offer of grace. And yet, when they reject it they do not topple God's throne. They do not take Him by surprise. Even their rebellion somehow serves His purpose.

But what of those who believe? What is Christ to them? Peter cites a passage from Isaiah as his answer. God promises to lay in Zion "a cornerstone, chosen and precious." To believe is to see Christ in that light—as precious, the pearl of great price, the gift of supreme value. Have you ever thought of faith in this way, as seeing things from God's perspective, as adjusting our values to His? God has made Jesus both Lord and Christ; faith says in response, "My Lord . . . you are the Christ." God speaks from heaven, "This is my beloved Son"; faith echoes, "Truly this was the Son of God." And just as God has "highly exalted him," so believing hearts cry, "Worthy is the Lamb that was slain." To you, therefore, who believe, He is precious.

And you have believed, haven't you? You have found Christ to be of inestimable worth. What then? Peter says, "Come to him." "But," you say, "I did that long ago." Yes, but Peter uses a present participle here, implying that we are always to be coming to Jesus Christ, turning our lives toward Him, responding to His call. And this ever renewed approach to Christ has a goal in view. "Like living stones, be yourselves built into a spiritual house." Did you note that sudden shift in terminology? Now Christians themselves are described as "living stones." As believers come into vital relationship with Jesus Christ and build their lives on Him, they partake of His life. And thus the structure of the church begins to rise— solid, enduring, yet vibrantly alive. Here is one more way of saying what the New Testament insists on by several images: Christians are in vital union with Christ and with each other.

Now the building metaphor has served its purpose. Peter wants to bring out something more about the new fellowship which we find in Christ. We are to "be a holy priesthood, to offer spiritual sacrifices acceptable to God through Jesus Christ." Once a select group within Israel served as priests; now all Christians fulfill that ministry. The Old Testament priests offered bulls and goats and rams in an elaborate sacrificial system; priests of the new covenant also have something to offer—something quite different. Since Christ Himself has made the supreme offering for sin, atoning sacrifices are no longer needed. The offerings which a Christian brings are all in grateful response to God's mercy. The Christian priest presents his "body as a living sacrifice," his whole life as an offering to God. He presents also hymns of praise, deeds of lowly ministry, acts of sharing, and prayers for the needs of others. These are his "spiritual sacrifices," and they all find favor with God through "that living stone," chosen and precious—Jesus Christ our Lord.

Chapter Nine

somebody special

*But you are a chosen race, a royal priesthood, a
holy nation, God's own people, that you may
declare the wonderful deeds of him who called you
out of darkness into his marvelous light. Once you
were no people but now you are God's people;
once you had not received mercy but now you
have received mercy* (I Peter 2:9-10, RSV).

How do you feel about yourself? Are you "somebody
special"—a person of real worth and importance? Be careful
how you answer that one. A negative answer may seem
humble and virtuous, but it is not. A positive response may
look like egotism of the worst sort, but it is not. In fact,
believing that you are "somebody" is crucial for your well-
being as a person.

To see the truth of that, consider the alternative for a
moment. Suppose that you think you are a "nobody"—
insignificant to yourself or to anyone else. If you feel that
way, life for you will be a grim business. It will be hard for
you to believe that anyone could care about you or that
anything you do could be worthwhile. What incentive will
you have then? And what can you ever give to anyone else?

This is the heartbreak, the tragedy, of the unloved or
unwanted child. Made painfully aware that no one cares
about him, he becomes sure that he isn't worth caring about.
Here is the pathos of many a ghetto youth, of the mentally
retarded, of the handicapped child. He has experienced rejec-

37

tion, defeat, and failure so many times that the message comes through to him loud and clear—"You're nobody. You just don't count." And so he retreats into his shell. Unrespected, he cannot show respect; unappreciated, he is powerless to appreciate; unloved, he remains unloving and alone.

What a service it is, what a ministry of love, when we can help someone like that to gain a sense of worth!

God did that for Israel. Before He led them out of Egypt, they were only slaves. You could hardly call them a people. They had no sense of national identity, no pride in who they were. Even the desire to be free had been slowly squeezed out of them. They were the least and the lowest. But when Moses had led them to the mount of God, this message came to them from the Lord: "You have seen what I did to the Egyptians and how I bore you on eagles' wings and brought you to myself. Now therefore if you will obey my voice and keep my covenant you shall be my own possession among all peoples; for all the earth is mine, and you shall be to me a kingdom of priests and a holy nation." That's what made Israel a people. The Lord most high had made a covenant with them. They were special because they were His.

Many centuries later, Peter echoed those words when he wrote to his fellow Christians. All the titles, all the privileges of ancient Israel now were theirs. They, too, were God's covenant people, precious in His sight. Among all the nations of the world they were a uniquely "chosen race." As Christians they shared in Christ's kingly reign, and as "priests" they represented all their fellowmen before the presence of God. They were "a holy nation" in the sense that God had set them apart for a special role in His eternal purpose. And more than that, they were "God's own people," privileged to belong to Him, to live in fellowship with Him, to know His Fatherly love. And remember, many of these first century Christians were slaves; very few were learned or wealthy or high-born. In the eyes of their contemporaries, most of them were nonentities. Think what it meant to them to find out who they really were!

But don't leave it in the past tense. This overwhelming good news is true for us, too. True today. We are still the covenant people. We who name Christ's name have a very significant place in His plan. Ponder that for a while. Savor it until the wonder of this "belonging" begins to sink in.

Peter's words make clear, though, that we owe all this to God's amazing mercy. We once were in darkness, groping blindly, aimless and lost. But God called us through His Son into "marvelous light." Once we were "no people" because, like many in Israel, we had spurned what we knew of God's light and love. We were "without God and without hope in the world." But now things are different and we are His people. Once we had not received mercy; once we lived under the shadow of God's wrath, exposed to His judgment through our ingratitude and rebellion. But now in Christ we are the forgiven ones, the redeemed, the beloved. "Rejoice in what you are," Peter seems to say, "but remember it is God's kindness that made you that way."

All right, then. Let's say that you take Peter's word seriously. You know that you are somebody special. Is that the end of it? For some, it seems to be. We are happy to know that we are among the chosen and that we are so important to God. But somehow that awareness brings with it no sense of responsibility, no urgency of obligation. When that happens, we've misunderstood what all these titles mean. We've failed to ask the question, "Why?" But once we've realized what our gifts and privileges are, that is the vital question to ask. Why are we chosen, holy and special? Peter's answer leaves no room for doubt: "that you may declare the wonderful deeds of him who called you out of darkness into his marvelous light."

I know a truck driver who made a remarkable discovery. Before his conversion to Christ he had often asked himself, "What are people for?" As he looked about him during long hours on the road, he could understand what the sun was for, and the rain. He could see a reason for the trees, the flowers, and for all the beauty which men can enjoy. But what about people? What are they for? He never understood that until, in Christ, he learned that we are for God—that we are made to praise Him.

But praising Him can never be just a private matter, can it?

Those who truly praise God cannot be content to keep what they know of Him to themselves. Having discovered how great and gracious He is, they want all the world to know. They want everything that has breath to praise Him. And so they tell His "wonderful deeds." They declare the glad news of what He has done for men in Jesus Christ. They tell of Bethlehem and the incredible stooping to share our life. They tell of Galilee and Jerusalem—deeds of compassion, words of life. They tell what God bore on Golgotha and how He triumphed on Easter morning. They tell of the first Pentecost and of all the others that stretch down into our own time. That's what people are for—to be God's heralds, God's announcers, His witnesses to all the world.

And they do it with more than words. The words are there—they have to be. But sometimes it's not the word that gets through first. Peter remembered the command of his Lord, "Let your light so shine before men that they may see your good works and glorify your Father which is in heaven." Yes, "show forth" His praises, as the Authorized Version puts it. Let them see His glory in your self-giving. Give them a glimpse of His love as you serve among them. The twofold formula for witness is a simple one. You learned it in your first days at school: "show and tell."

Christians, God says you're "somebody" all right—somebody special. But you're never somebody for yourself alone. It's always for Him—and for them.

Chapter Ten

a plea for character

Beloved, I beseech you as aliens and exiles to abstain from the passions of the flesh that wage war against your soul. Maintain good conduct among the Gentiles, so that in case they speak against you as wrongdoers, they may see your good deeds and glorify God on the day of visitation (I Peter 2:11-12, RSV).

"Does it make any difference how I live?" If the question sounds ridiculous to us, we may be out of touch with our time. For many are raising questions like that—raising them seriously. We live in an age when moral issues have become increasingly blurred, when "right" and "wrong" have been almost emptied of meaning for multitudes. Moreover, many of these same people see morality (whatever that means now) as a purely private affair: "My personal life is my own business and no one else's."

Nothing could be further removed from the thought world of the Bible. From the standpoint of Christian faith, how we live is tremendously important, both to us and to those around us. Listen to the apostle Peter as he makes an impassioned plea for Christian character. "Beloved, I beseech you . . . to abstain from the passions of the flesh."

Striking, isn't it, how he approaches his fellow Christians? This is an apostle of Christ, an eyewitness of His sufferings, a divinely authorized teacher of the church. Yet there is nothing authoritarian about his approach to people. Peter is no drill sergeant, barking orders to the Christian army. Rather, he speaks to them as "beloved," and his words of exhortation are more an entreaty than a command. "But Peter, you're demeaning yourself," someone objects. "Where is your authority as an apostle?" Apparently Peter felt that love and a spirit of meekness were not inconsistent with apostolic authority. Where do you suppose he got that idea?

Beneath this tenderness throbs an urgent concern. "Abstain from the passions of the flesh," pleads Peter. What does he mean? It is easy to slide over that latter phrase too quickly. To most readers, the words have a narrow range of meaning—applying chiefly, if not entirely, to sexual license. But "flesh" in the New Testament has no such restricted meaning. It stands for the totality of our human nature, marred and infected as it is by sin. The "passions of the flesh" may be sensual cravings, but they may also take the form of greed or inordinate ambition or the lust for power. What then—are natural human urges to be squelched? Is it virtuous to be passionless? No, the apostle certainly doesn't mean that. But these human desires, wholesome and good in themselves, can become occasions of evil when misused. Suppose a desire runs unchecked and gains the mastery over us or is directed toward a wrong object. Or perhaps it is satisfied at the expense of someone else. Then it becomes a "passion of the flesh"—something to restrain and shun.

So you like to eat. It is perfectly normal that you should; God made you that way. But if because of some emotional problem—some unfulfilled personal need—you eat to an excess which threatens your health, that desire has become a positive menace. Again, your longing for sexual fulfillment is God given. But when that desire is directed toward another's partner, a Christian must resist and redirect it. And if your desires for security or pleasure or property drive you to exploit other persons, they are no longer wholesome.

Peter first bases his appeal for character on who these Christians are: "as aliens and exiles." He takes it for granted that to be ruled by one's passions is the customary thing in this world. This is the way we all live, by nature. As Isaiah so vividly put it: "We have turned every one to his own way."

But Christians have been redeemed from the tyranny of this present age; they have known the transforming power of Christ. In Him they have a higher citizenship, a nobler pattern for living. Though they are very much a part of life in this world and are meant to be deeply involved in it, they are at the same time detached from its values and standards. This world is not their final home nor their ultimate reference point. They belong to the risen Lord who is making all things new. Therefore, as "aliens and exiles," let them never conform again to the old way of life.

The apostle's next reason is a very practical one. He wants Christians to abstain from the passions of the flesh because of their harmful effects. They "wage war against your soul." They are the enemies of your Christian growth. Enslaving passions deny Christ's lordship over us. They make idolaters of us, setting up other objects for our worship. They strive against the work of the Spirit, who is seeking to produce in us the likeness of Christ. A person's runaway desire can be his worst enemy.

But there is a third great reason for developing Christian character. "Maintain good conduct among the Gentiles," urges Peter. Remember that you live in the midst of unbelievers. They watch your lives. True, they may speak against you even when your conduct is blameless. They may slander and misjudge you for your efforts to follow Christ. But no matter—let your conduct among them be "good." (The word means, literally, "beautiful." Remember what Iago said of Cassio in Shakespeare's tragedy? "He hath a daily beauty in his life that makes me ugly.") Christian character has a winsomeness about it which impresses even the most skeptical. And a practical obedience to Christ, a daily living by His law of servant-love, can have redemptive effects. Peter seems to say that those who slander and scoff at Christians may one day have a change of heart. Seeing the good deeds of believers, they may "glorify God on the day of visitation." That is, when God speaks to them, when Christ confronts them in the gospel, when their hearts become open to His call, they will praise God for those Christians who "lived Christ" among them.

What a wonderfully encouraging thought! Christian character witnesses powerfully to the living Lord. When believers
curb passions of the flesh and manifest a Christlike character, the gospel gains a hearing. Our Savior promised that,
didn't He? "Let your light so shine before men that they may
see your good works and glorify your Father which is in
heaven."

Chapter Eleven

patriotic or christian?

Be subject for the Lord's sake to every human institution, whether it be to the emperor as supreme, or to governors as sent by him to punish those who do wrong and to praise those who do right. For it is God's will that by doing right you should put to silence the ignorance of foolish men. Live as free men, yet without using your freedom as a pretext for evil; but live as servants of God. Honor all men. Love the brotherhood. Fear God. Honor the emperor (I Peter 2:13-17, RSV).

Should we be patriotic or should we be Christian? Would you believe that Christians in the United States could be divided over a question like that? As a matter of fact, they are. Not that there are any who say that we ought not to be Christian! On that, at least, we all agree. The division arises over whether or not the first question is a live issue. There are some, for example, who see here no occasion of conflict. For them, Christianity has become so closely identified with "the American way of life" that they see little difference between the two. It is assumed that being Christian and being loyally American cover pretty much the same ground.

At the other pole are people who believe that United States policy is often in sharp conflict with the claims and spirit of the gospel. On questions like the war in Vietnam or civil rights, for example, there are those who believe that being patriotic and being Christian are irreconcilable alternatives. We all know of contemporary churchmen who have publicly defied the claims of government by appeal to the Biblical faith.

This tension within the church was brought into clear focus at a recent General Synod meeting of the Reformed Church in America, held in Ann Arbor, Michigan. Under the general heading "War, Draft, and Conscience," the Christian Action Commission brought the following recommendation before Synod: "We recommend, therefore, that the General Synod reaffirm the fact that the first loyalty of a Christian is to the lordship of Jesus Christ both in private and public living, and that dissent from public policy when based upon conviction is legitimate and necessary." Here the issue is clearly raised: Christ above country. An amendment was then proposed that after the word "living," the following should be added: "and under that lordship he has a loyalty to his country to whose military service he may be called." This point of view was willing to affirm Christ's supreme lordship, but insisted that this involves no conflict with patriotism. The strange division of the church was later displayed in the fact that the amendment *and* the original motion were defeated!

What do we make of this? How should the Christian see his relationship to civil government?

The apostle Peter grappled with the same issue in the first century. The government under which he lived was vastly different from ours, of course; yet his teaching has surprising relevance to our situation. His first word is a clear call to civil obedience: "Be subject . . . to every human institution, whether it be to the emperor as supreme or to governors as sent by him." It could hardly be plainer. Put in contemporary terms, it means that Christians are to obey the law of the land, whether on a federal, state, or local level. From the Supreme Court to the traffic court, from income tax to parking regulations, believers are to be subject to duly constituted authority. The witness of our Lord and His apostles is consistent on this basic principle (cf. Matt. 22:21, Rom. 13:1-7).

But while they say this clearly, it is not all they have to say. Note how Peter adds the significant phrase, "for the Lord's sake." Here he is saying something about the motivation for civil obedience. The Christian is to be governed not merely by the fear of punishment nor by social convention, but by conscience toward God. Here Peter is implying what Paul states explicitly in Romans 13:1: "The governing authorities . . . have been instituted by God." This does not mean, of course, that each political regime conforms to God's will. But it does mean that God wills institutional government as over against anarchy. One existing government may not be better than another, but it is almost always better than no government at all.

In order to understand Peter, we need to see that he is thinking of human authority in this general sense. He speaks of it as a system designed "to punish those who do wrong and to praise those who do right." Now, he certainly knew that not every decree of the Roman emperor had those precise effects. But he did see that the total system tended to secure such ends. And is there not a fairly large common core in every governmental system which all of its citizens recognize as just? It is obviously that kind of law or regulation which Peter has in mind when he calls for obedience. "For it is God's will," he contends, "that *by doing right* you should put to silence the ignorance of foolish men."

Apparently the early Christians were sometimes considered as lawbreakers. Peter is deeply concerned that they should not bring down that charge on themselves by any wrongdoing. He is insisting on a kind of conduct that will adorn the gospel. Careless men will always speak ignorantly against Christians, but Peter says, "Put them to shame—put them to silence—'muzzle' them" (the literal translation) by a life that is above reproach. He simply warns against being less just, less honest, less responsible than our non-Christian neighbors. If we are, how can we possibly point them to Christ?

But when all this has been said, it needs to be pointed out that Peter is not calling for a blind, unquestioning submission to civil government. In fact, he directly asserts that believers are "free men"; they are never to be the slaves and dupes of any system. Christ has redeemed them. A Christian man is, in Luther's words, "a perfectly free man, subject to none." He is freed from the shackles of evil in his own life and from the suffocating pressures of group conformity. And yet he must never use that wonderful freedom "as a pretext for evil." His new freedom is not license—not a liberty to scout all authority and to trample over people. Rather, says the apostle, "Live as servants of God." Live as those who belong totally to God, whose consciences are wholly bound by His will.

And so before we put Peter on the side of those who oppose all civil disobedience, we need to give due weight to that phrase, "live as servants of God." The apostle is not discussing here a situation in which the claims of God and the claims of government come into conflict. But when that situation did arise in his own experience, he had no hesitation about making the choice. "We must obey God rather than men" (Acts 5:29). Luther, also, could resist the highest civil and religious authority of his day with the claim, "My conscience is bound by the Word of God." It is always a serious thing to defy human government, and a man needs to be very sure of his Biblical warrant when he does so. But there come times when loyalty to God's will requires it. As the apostle Paul wisely said in another connection: "Let everyone be fully convinced in his own mind."

Finally, we are to "honor all men," seeing each human being created in God's image as entitled to our respect. We are to love with a special love the "brotherhood" of those who belong to Christ. And, Peter concludes, we ought both to fear God and to honor earthly rulers. To this thorny issue of conflicting loyalties, the apostle is really applying the incomparable answer of his Lord: "Render therefore to Caesar the things that are Caesar's and to God the things that are God's."

Chapter Twelve

when your boss is impossible

> *Servants, be submissive to your masters with all
> respect, not only to the kind and gentle but also to
> the overbearing. For one is approved if, mindful of
> God, he endures pain while suffering unjustly. For
> what credit is it, if when you do wrong and are
> beaten for it you take it patiently? But if when
> you do right and suffer for it you take it patiently,
> you have God's approval. For to this you have
> been called, because Christ also suffered for you,
> leaving you an example, that you should follow in
> his steps. He committed no sin; no guile was found
> on his lips. When he was reviled, he did not revile
> in return; when he suffered, he did not threaten,
> but he trusted to him who judges justly* (I Peter
> 2:18-23, RSV).

When your boss is the most insensitive person alive, when
your superior is a petty dictator, or when your coach rides
you unmercifully, how do you react? Maybe you decide to
quit and go elsewhere; that's one way to get around it. Or
perhaps you give him a piece of your mind and get fired;
that's another way. Or maybe you conceal and nurse your
bitterness, cursing the enemy when he is well out of earshot.
But somehow none of these responses seems wholly satis-
fying, does it? At least, not to a Christian.

Simon Peter, special messenger of Jesus Christ, recom-
mends another approach. It may seem hard to take in, but

here it is: "Be submissive to your masters with all respect, not only to the kind and gentle, but also to the overbearing." He actually addressed these words to household servants, but in a real sense they apply to anyone who does his work under human authority. Peter's formula is this: submit to his orders and show him all respect, not only if he's a "good Joe," but even if he's the worst creep imaginable (that word translated "overbearing" literally means "crooked"—maybe he's even that bad).

"But," comes the objection, "you don't know the misery that guy has caused me." But apparently Peter did. He knew that some of the servants to whom he was writing had endured physical beatings—treatment probably a good deal rougher than any we have experienced. And still they were to carry out the wishes of these taskmasters, treating them with the utmost respect. Sounds impossible, doesn't it? Or even stupid. Who's dumb enough to be a doormat?

But foolish as this kind of conduct may seem, Peter claims that it has God's approval. That does not mean, of course, that He is pleased with just any kind of trouble we get into on the job. If we are honest about it, we will have to admit that sometimes we bring our difficulties on ourselves. If we are obnoxious or always late, or if we don't hustle in basketball practice, we are naturally going to be reprimanded—maybe even penalized. And that doesn't make us particularly noble. As Peter puts it, "What credit is it, if when you do wrong and are beaten for it you take it patiently?" Anyone should take that kind of treatment patiently. We simply got what was coming to us. The kind of thing that wins God's approval is quite different. Here is a situation where a servant is doing his level best to please his master. Suddenly, just because the boss happens to be in a foul mood and takes out his grouch on this poor servant, some real suffering results. Peter says, when that occurs and a servant bears it patiently without bitterness, God says, "Thank you."

Now there are certain conclusions which we ought *not* to draw from this. One of them is that disagreeable bosses are excused for what they do. Peter certainly does not mean to give comfort to any tyrant of an employer. The Bible fairly throbs with a divine indignation against those who misuse authority and heartlessly exploit people. If Peter had a word to say to unjust masters, it would surely sound this note.

Nor is the apostle legislating for every kind of work relationship. The average worker today has a great deal more going for him than did a typical first century servant. He has far greater freedom and mobility. Through collective bargaining he has powerful allies to help him plead his cause. If Peter had been writing to the working classes in the last third of the twentieth century, he certainly would not say that labor's only Christian response to injustice is to submit to it. But the point was that these servants were powerless to correct the situation in which they were placed. And often today, even though labor has made great strides in recent decades, situations still arise in which an individual worker or employee feels trapped. He is being treated unjustly, but he needs the job and he can't fight the system. For the time being, at least, he has to live with it. Peter's words are meant for him.

It is not that the apostle favors an abject submission as over against, say, arbitration or a considered complaint. He is working at the deeper level of personal attitude. What he is saying is that *anyone* can pay back in kind—good service for fair treatment, or bitter defiance in exchange for abuse. But a Christian is called to something more than that. Peter had the words of his own Master ringing in his ears: "If you love those who love you, what credit is that to you . . . and if you do good to those who do good to you, what credit is that to you? For even sinners do the same . . . but love your enemies and do good . . . and your reward will be great and you will be sons of the Most High, for he is kind to the ungrateful and the selfish." There it is, a new kind of life breaking into human history. A brand new possibility—so that someone else's hate doesn't have to get inside of us and turn us sour—so that we can begin to meet ugliness with love.

And Peter knows that this new life is not a dream, not a misty ideal. He has seen it in action. He has seen it "with skin on." Hear his charge to these Christians: "For to this you have been called, because Christ also suffered for you, leaving you an example that you should follow in his steps." Here is the open secret: This is the way Christ lived. He suffered on behalf of unlovely people; He bore agony for the very ones who rejected and scorned and murdered Him. And He has left us "an example." That word "example" can mean the "tracing" of letters for children to write over or copy, or it can mean an artist's sketch, left to be colored in by others. With either figure the message is plain. Here is a model which the master artist has provided for us beginners to work at.

How did our Lord react to harsh treatment? How did He respond when He was manhandled and insulted by petty authorities? "He committed no sin": He did nothing wrong. "No guile was found on his lips": He made no attempt to deceive, to talk His way out of trouble by cunning. When He was sneered at, He had no answering sneers. When He suffered at the hands of men, He did not menace them with threats or call down heaven's vengeance on them. Rather, He committed His cause to the one Judge who is altogether just. Suffering unjustly, suffering in love, He was able to leave the matter in God's hands and pray, "Father, forgive them."

We want to follow this Christ, don't we? This, at least, is what we say. But are we really ready for this? Following in His steps can seem very adventuresome until it means enduring shame and pain from petty people. Then the glamour has clean gone out of it. But when we can absorb that kind of treatment and still go on loving, leaving our case with God, *that* is discipleship.

Chapter Thirteen

the death of jesus:
its meaning for us

He himself bore our sins in his body on the tree, that we might die to sin and live to righteousness. By his wounds you have been healed. For you were straying like sheep, but have now returned to the Shepherd and Guardian of your souls (I Peter 2:24-25, RSV).

What meaning does the death of Jesus have for your life? Perhaps you see it as *tragedy*. Well, you are in good company there. Simon Peter, the leader of the apostles, once felt that way about it too. When Jesus first began to speak of His death, Peter was horrified. He would hear nothing of it. "God forbid, Lord," he cried; "this will never happen to you." And, like all the other disciples, he was numb with grief and despair when his Master was finally crucified. As he watched that sordid scene on Golgotha, he saw in it nothing but gloom and loss. But Easter morning changed all that. Peter saw things then in a different light.

It may be that you have seen in Jesus' death a *noble example*. So did Peter. He held it up as a pattern for all to follow, particularly those who suffer unjustly. Here is one who endured terrible wrongs, though He Himself had never wronged anyone. See how He bore it, says Peter; and follow in His steps. See Him praying for His enemies and committing His soul to God. Learn from Jesus Christ how to die.

Perhaps you are one of those who see in Christ a *martyr* dying for a cause. And you have seen rightly. The word from which our word *martyr* comes means "witness." Jesus proclaimed Himself as a witness to the truth of God, as one who represented God's cause upon the earth. Because of what He taught, because of what He stood for, because of what He was, men opposed and threatened Him. But He was not cowed by their threatenings, nor would He retract a word of His testimony. He chose death rather than compromise. As Peter put it, "He simply committed his cause to the One who judges fairly."

But some of you see more than this in Jesus' death. You see here a powerful *moral influence*. And Peter saw that too. In his words, Jesus gave His life "that we might die to sin and live to righteousness." Peter was convinced that Jesus' dying was meant to make a difference in our living. And it does, wherever people begin to grasp its meaning. What—is sin such a terrible reality in human hearts that it even crucifies God's Son? Then surely we cannot tolerate it in our lives. If it caused Him to die, then we must die to it—renounce it— have nothing more to do with it. And just as He rose from the dead, so are we henceforth to live a new kind of life. Jesus' obedience to God's will, even unto death, summons us also to obey.

But there is a meaning in the cross which transcends all these others and which lends to each its peculiar power. Have you seen *Christ dying in your place?* Hear how Peter describes it: "He himself bore our sins in his body on the tree." The idea of bearing sin is a familiar one in the Old Testament. To bear sin means to bear the punishment for it, to suffer the consequences of it (Lev. 20:20; Num. 18:22). Peter is saying here that Jesus endured what we deserve. "In his body," as a flesh-and-blood man, He went through death for us. The apostle's use of the word "tree" for the cross makes this meaning especially clear. He is speaking not merely as an eyewitness to the crucifixion, but also as one who knows this somber word from the Old Testament: "His body shall not remain all night upon the tree, but you shall bury him the same day, *for a hanged man is accursed by God.*" In some way beyond our power to grasp, our curse, our condemnation, was borne by Jesus Christ.

How did Peter ever get this idea about Jesus' death? True, it was foreshadowed in Isaiah 53, but Peter never saw the connection during the days of Jesus' ministry. The Lord Himself had hinted at it, but Peter always missed the point. No, it was not the crucifixion itself, but the risen Christ who made this plain to the apostles. It was He who taught them from the Old Testament the things concerning Himself. From Him they learned that "Christ died for our sins according to the Scriptures." And this amazing event, interpreted by the risen Lord Himself, became their gospel. They felt the constraint of God's Spirit to proclaim it to every man.

But Peter is not writing here to those who have never heard this message. He writes to Christians, God's own people. To them the word of Christ crucified comes as a reminder: "By his wounds you have been healed." Here is the glorious, positive side of the truth. Christ bore our sins: His sufferings have saved us, His pain has made us free, His death has given us life. "You were straying like sheep," continues Peter. You were away from your true home, estranged from your rightful Lord, wandering, lost, in peril. But now through Christ's death you have "returned" to the Shepherd and Guardian of your souls.

Here Peter speaks from personal experience. He had known what it was to wander away, to prove false, to deny his Master. But Jesus had promised that he would return (literally, "be converted"), and return he did. Now he was obeying the charge of his Lord, "when you have turned again, strengthen your brethren" (Luke 22:32).

"But what great difference does it make," asks someone, "how we understand the cross?" If all these meanings can be found in it, why not, as the saying goes, "pay your money and take your choice"? The answer is that no one of these meanings (or no combination of them, for that matter), if taken without the last, can call forth the faith with which the New Testament is vibrantly alive. I may admire Jesus' example and honor His martyrdom and even be moved by His death to moral improvement, and yet miss the heart of New Testament Christianity. It is only when I realize that my sins caused Him to die and that He willingly bore them for me, that I begin to know the good news of God's love. The characteristic note of early Christianity was not first of all a heroic attempt to emulate Christ. That vision came—and must come—but it always came second. First came the sense of immeasurable debt to the crucified Lord. Wonder, trust, and grateful love are born with this conviction: "He loved me and gave himself for me."

Chapter Fourteen

a winsome wife

*Likewise you wives, be submissive to your hus-
bands, so that some, though they do not obey the
word, may be won without a word by the behavior
of their wives, when they see your reverent and
chaste behavior. Let not yours be the outward
adorning with braiding of hair, decoration of gold,
and wearing of robes, but let it be the hidden
person of the heart with the imperishable jewel of
a gentle and quiet spirit, which in God's sight is
very precious. So once the holy women who hoped
in God used to adorn themselves and were submissive to their husbands, as Sarah obeyed Abraham,
calling him lord. And you are now her children if
you do right and let nothing terrify you* (I Peter
3:1-6, RSV).

"Wives, be submissive to your husbands." What do we
make of a command like that? At this juncture in history,
after all the progress we have witnessed in women's rights, is
there room any longer for a call to domestic submission? This
sort of thing may have been all right for the ancient world,
but can any self-respecting woman accept it today?

These are questions not to be lightly dismissed. Women
occupy a vastly different situation in modern society than
they did when Peter wrote to his contemporaries. They have
shown their ability to compete successfully with men in one
field of endeavor after another. And few would argue that

their objection to domestic tyranny is anything but wholesome and right.

Before we conclude, however, that Peter's word to wives is hopelessly outdated, let's look carefully at what he means by "submission." Notice, for example, that this command is part of a long section in which he urges several different groups to "be subject." Citizens, for example, are to be subject to human authority, and servants to their masters. In neither case is it assumed that this submission implies inferiority. Rulers may be foolish and employers obnoxious, but still they are to be shown due respect. The Christian is urged to be submissive "for the Lord's sake."

It is significant also that after his word to wives, Peter calls on husbands to treat their partners with consideration and honor. He plainly does not intend to degrade womanhood or to encourage male dictatorship.

Well, what does the apostle mean by submissive? If it isn't debasing servitude, what is it? Perhaps we find a clue in the type of behavior which Peter later urges wives to manifest. They are to be "chaste and reverent." The word translated "chaste" here means, literally, "pure." The wife is to be utterly faithful to her husband—free from uncleanness in all her manner of living. And she is to be "reverent," living with the awareness that she is responsible to God, conscious always of His presence. Also, she is to manifest "a calm and gentle spirit." Let there be nothing loud and abrasive about her, but rather a sweet reasonableness, a gentle dignity. Monica, the mother of Augustine, was a remarkable model of this. "She knew that a woman must not resist a husband in anger, by deed or even by word. Only, when she saw him calm again and quiet she would take the opportunity to give him an explanation of her action if it happened that he had been roused to anger unreasonably."

Finally, Peter sums up wifely submission in these words: "Do good and show no fear." True submission never means cowering dread of a husband, never a cooperation born of fright. Rather, the submission of a Christian wife chiefly means doing good to her husband, showing love for him in practical, down-to-earth ways. And servant-love can never be demeaning, not since the Lord of glory came among us "as one who serves."

The wife who lives with her husband in this way will be a winning witness. In fact, Peter indicates that unbelieving husbands—even those who seem hardened to the gospel message—can often be converted through the agency of their wives. It is not that the wife is more effective in explaining the gospel than the minister or evangelist. It is her translation of the gospel into life—right before the man's eyes—which proves a telling witness. See how God honored it in the case of Monica. Augustine writes of her in his *Confessions*: "When she reached the age for marriage and was bestowed upon a husband, she served him as her lord. She used all her effort to win him to You, preaching You to him by her character, by which You made her beautiful to her husband, respected and loved by him and admirable in his sight . . . . The upshot was that towards the very end of his life she won her husband to You . . . ."

Did you notice that Augustine said that her character made her beautiful to her husband? Peter sees this as the second great result of submission. There is a beauty which consists chiefly in outward adornment—"the braiding of the hair, or jewelry, or dress." Peter does not mean to condemn this. What he urges, however, is that a woman's time and attention should be focused mainly on the acquiring of another kind of beauty: "the unfading loveliness of a calm and gentle spirit" (v. 4, Phillips). This is the winsome beauty that wears well, the beauty that delights God's heart as well as the heart of a husband. It would be disappointing, of course, if women were to concentrate so exclusively on "inner beauty" that they neglected their outward appearance. Peter is hardly recommending that. But is it not far sadder when a wife's concern for loveliness of attire, or of face and form, outruns her desire to be a lovely person?

Best of all, the submission of a Christian wife reveals her trust in God. According to Peter, it has always been this way. "Thus it was among God's people in days of old: the women who fixed their hopes on him adorned themselves by submission to their husbands" (v. 5, NEB). The wife sees in her husband something of God's own rule and grace. She, his beloved, looks to him as a God given protector, provider, and source of help. In that sense she obeys him and calls him her "lord." Being a devoted wife becomes a part—and no small part—of a woman's grateful service to God.

Such living marks a woman, Peter maintains, as a true descendant of Sarah, Abraham's wife. To follow in the footsteps of Abraham is to share his faith in God's promise; to follow in Sarah's is to put that faith into operation within the home. Christian submission for a wife really boils down to a rather simple formula: Trust in God and love your husband.

Chapter Fifteen

husbands "in the know"

Likewise, ye husbands, dwell with them according to knowledge, giving honour unto the wife, as unto the weaker vessel, and as being heirs together of the graces of life; that your prayers be not hindered (I Peter 3:7, AV).

What does a man most need to know in order to be a good husband? Scientific data on sex? A course in the mysteries of female psychology? Or is it hints in the subtle art of lovemaking?

No doubt all of these would prove helpful. But there is another type of education which is more crucial than any of them for the highest success of a husband. When the apostle Peter urges husbands to dwell with their wives "according to knowledge" he means, at the deepest level, the knowledge of *God*. He is writing to men who name Christ's name, urging them to apply what they know of God in Christ to the way they treat their wives.

That other great apostle, Paul, put it this way: "Husbands, love your wives as Christ loved the church and gave himself for her." In other words, the marvelous love of God, revealed and given to us in Jesus Christ, is to be the husband's model. This is to guide and control every aspect of his homelife. The "highest that we know" is our Savior's self-giving love, even unto death. The Christian husband can hear his Lord say, "Love her as I have loved you."

But how does this work itself out in the daily life of the

family? Peter suggests that we think of it as "giving honor unto the wife." How much respect, esteem, consideration, and courtesy is included in that! The husband gives honor to his wife when he remembers to be thoughtful in little ways. He gives her honor when he tries to understand her feelings and takes time to listen when she longs to talk. He honors her when he refrains from belittling or blaming her in the presence of others. He gives her honor in the intimate relationships of married life by prizing her fulfillment at least as much as his own. He honors her by the timely word of praise and appreciation that makes her whole day bright. And on every day, he honors her with a kind of reverence—seeing in her a unique and wonderful person whom it is a privilege to know and to love.

But Peter, being a family man himself, knows how hard it is for husbands to live this way. He knows how most of us are all too often selfish and inconsiderate. And so, to spur us on toward what we ought to be, he leaves us with three good reasons for giving honor to our wives.

First, the wife is "the weaker vessel." Now in some respects, that's hard to believe. There is much that seems to prove otherwise, even if we don't believe those stories about the Amazons. Who lives longer? Who has fewer heart attacks? And who, in some societies, just about runs the whole show? You know who, and it isn't *he*! But for the most part, women *are* physically weaker than men (at least men's Olympic records are better than theirs) and perhaps not as well fitted to carry some of the heavier burdens and responsibilities of life. And this, says Peter, is the reason they ought to be honored.

What a strange outlook! Isn't it strength that demands respect, rather than weakness? Aren't the weak to be dominated, used, and held in contempt by the strong? Sad to say, it's often that way. But not among followers of Christ. Nietzsche despised Christianity because of its compassion for the weak, afflicted, and handicapped, but what he sniffed at is still the glory of the gospel. Peter appeals here to a noble use of strength. The husband is the "house-band"—the strong encircling arms that hold a home together. Let a wife's weakness be a call to his manhood. In God's eyes, he proves himself a man not when he lords it over her, but when he becomes her strength and shield.

Here is a second weighty reason: husbands are to honor their wives "as being heirs together of the grace of life." "Heirs together"—what a lovely phrase. It reminds the husband that he and his wife are bound together in the bundle of life. They are one flesh, sharers of one life. For a husband to injure his wife is sheer madness. The man who does that is like a maniac who maims his own body. For he who wrongs his wife wrongs the best part of himself. To despise your wife is to despise yourself. To degrade her is to degrade yourself. To give her joy is to fill your own cup to overflowing. "He who loves his wife," says Paul, "loves himself."

There is something else implied in the words "heirs together" or "fellow heirs." Whether the "grace of life" described here is simply the wonder of life in this world, or whether it means the inbreaking of eternal life through Jesus Christ, the fact remains that husband and wife are *joint heirs*. They are equal before God, equally precious to the one who redeemed them. Let no husband imagine that because his wife is called to be submissive to him, she is therefore inferior. She is not. Let no husband ever see his wife as a second-class citizen in God's kingdom or as one whose spiritual life is less important than his own. Let him honor her as his beloved "fellow heir."

Now we are ready for Peter's last word to husbands. There is a deeper dimension involved in the commonplaces of domestic life. Husbands, urges the apostle, treat your wives with honor "that your prayers be not hindered." Mull over that for a while. Note first how Peter is assuming that these Christian husbands pray. An unfair assumption? Not really. To belong to Christ and to pray—these can hardly be separated. Believers are those who "call on the name of the Lord." If prayer is indeed "the Christian's vital breath," can there be life at all in the heart that never prays?

Peter chiefly notes, however, the close connection between domestic relationships and effectual prayer. So profound and significant is the bond between husband and wife that it affects every dimension of the life of both persons, including their relationship to God. Or perhaps we should say, *chiefly* their relationship to God. The teaching of Scripture is relentlessly consistent at this point. We cannot at one and the same time love God and hate our neighbors. Nor can husbands slight their wives and still draw near to God. Sometimes an apology to *her* may be in order before a petition to *Him*. The prayers of a surly husband can be nothing but a jarring noise to God.

But there is a positive side to this too, isn't there? If domestic discord can hinder our prayers, then what must love and unity do for them? What power there is, Jesus assures us, in the prayers of even two who agree together on earth! Husband, do you want your prayers for God's kingdom and for the true welfare of your children to count? Then live with your wife "according to knowledge"—in the light of Christ's love.

Chapter Sixteen

life under god's smile

Finally, all of you, have unity of spirit, sympathy, love of the brethren, a tender heart and a humble mind. Do not return evil for evil or reviling for reviling; but on the contrary bless, for to this you have been called, that you may obtain a blessing. For "He that would love life and see good days, let him keep his tongue from evil and his lips from speaking guile; let him turn away from evil and do right; let him seek peace and pursue it. For the eyes of the Lord are upon the righteous, and his ears are open to their prayer. But the face of the Lord is against those that do evil" (I Peter 3:8-12, RSV).

Think for a moment of the congregation to which you belong. What if all its members were like-minded, inclined to emphasize the great things you all have in common, maintaining openness and unity in the fellowship? And what if each was possessed of sympathy, able to share the feelings of others, rejoicing with the glad and weeping with those who weep? What if each loved everyone else with brotherly affection, recognizing and accepting him as a fellow child in God's family? What if each was tender-hearted, kind, swift to encourage and help? Yes, and what if each, together with these other graces, had a humble mind: a readiness to serve in lowly ways, a willingness to listen to and respect the contributions of others?

"Well," you say, "that's pleasant to dream about, but isn't it too much to expect? Our congregation certainly doesn't measure up." Quite right. And there are probably very few congregations that do. Yet this is the pattern of life which Peter sets before his Christian friends. This is what life in the new fellowship is meant to be. No doubt Peter's contemporaries hadn't fully arrived, either. But he still felt there was value in setting the standard before them. Perhaps we should not conclude too quickly that this kind of life is an unattainable ideal. Maybe your congregation isn't like this—certainly not completely. But it would be further along this very day if only one person (say, yourself) was to make it his fixed purpose to cultivate these graces. In a congregation, as in a marriage, there is only one person whom each of us can realistically hope to change, and you know who that is.

Now take an inventory of how you and your fellow Christians react to harsh treatment. When you are abused or slighted or mocked, when people take advantage of you or accuse you unjustly, what sort of response do you give? To make it very practical, what do you do when another driver cuts in front of you in heavy traffic or when someone steals your place in line after you've waited for an hour? When someone accused you of being a hippie or a Communist because you took what you felt was a Christian stand on some social issue, what happened? Regardless of what did happen, here is what the apostle Peter says *should* happen: "Do not return evil for evil, or reviling for reviling, but on the contrary, bless." There it is again, that miracle style of life. With most people, you reap what you sow. Shove them and they will shove back. Sow an insult and you will reap a choicer one. That's the age-old pattern, and it leads to mounting hate and violence. But the Christians whom Peter describes don't feed back what they receive. They don't merely answer in kind. Somehow they transform what comes at them, so that insults generate prayers and hate comes back as love.

Earlier, the apostle described the basis for this strange conduct. Christians are to respond to evil in this way because it is precisely how their Lord and Master responded. His example and His love provide the resources to break the vicious circle of hostility. Also, Peter had pointed to the profound effect which behavior like this has on unbelievers, sometimes leading to their conversion. Now he has something else to say to those who can endure hostile treatment and still manifest love: "For to this you have been called, that you may obtain a blessing." God in Christ has chosen and invited them to this kind of life, so that in living it they may inherit His blessing. Peter then enlarges upon what he means by appealing to the familiar lines of the 34th Psalm. They bring a strong assurance to God's servants. Those who keep evil and guile from their speech, who renounce the evil and do good, who long and labor for peace—they, says the psalmist, will be blessed. God's smile will be on them.

There are some Christians who are uncomfortable with this idea. So convinced are they that salvation is by grace, without any merit or striving of their own, that it rather pains them when the notion of reward is introduced. Ought not believers to serve God out of gratitude, they reason, without thinking of what they will get out of it? Others have trouble with the doctrine of divine blessing on the upright because, like Job, they don't seem to see it happening in this world. Yet here it is, the promise of God recorded again and again in Scripture that those who walk in the path of discipleship will inherit a blessing. How are we to understand this "blessing"?

First of all, it is obvious that neither material prosperity nor earthly success is the central focus of the promise. The godly will "love life" and they will "see good days" but they will sometimes despair of life, too, and pass through days that are dreary and desolating. Let Job and a host of others testify that God's attitude toward us cannot be determined by our outward circumstances.

Nor does the promise imply that good deeds can ever earn God's favor. The glad news of the gospel is that God loves us in spite of what we are, rather than because of it. Peter had heard from his Master that even when disciples have obeyed all of God's commands, they are still to say: "We are unworthy servants; we have only done what was our duty."

The fact remains, however, that God *has* promised to reward the patient endurance of His people. While we may urge one another not to serve merely for the sake of reward, it is hardly wise to blame God because He chooses to be gracious! Since He sets forth the hope of future blessing as a motive for faithfulness in trial, it would be sheer ingratitude and unbelief for us to despise it.

The heart of the promise is in these grand words: "The eyes of the Lord are upon the righteous and his ears are open to their prayer." Here is your reward, suffering Christian. Here is your strong consolation. The Lord sees you in the midst of your trouble, and His smile is upon you. He knows, He cares; and because He is ready to hear your cry, no prayer from the depths will go unanswered. He will never forsake you. So go on, blessed ones, returning good for evil and love for hate. Those who see the light on God's face can smile at anything.

Chapter Seventeen

when the pressure is on

*After all, who in the ordinary way is likely to
injure you for being enthusiastic for good? And if
it should happen that you suffer "for righteousness' sake," that is a privilege. You need neither
fear their threats nor worry about them; simply
concentrate on being completely devoted to Christ
in your hearts. Be ready at any time to give a quiet
and reverent answer to any man who wants a
reason for the hope that you have within you.
Make sure that your conscience is perfectly clear,
so that if men should speak slanderously of you as
rogues they may come to feel ashamed of themselves for libeling your good Christian behavior* (I
Peter 3:13-16, Phillips).

You are hated because you speak out against racism. You
are jeered at for choosing chastity in a promiscuous age. You
are branded as a "leftist" because you seek some needed
social change. You are rejected as "narrow" by the urbane
and sophisticated. At times like these, when the pressure is
on, what should a Christian do?

The apostle Peter has an answer, an answer he learned the
hard way. He had known the humiliation of folding up under
pressure, of failing his Lord completely. But once forgiven
and restored, he had taken even sterner testings in stride. He
knew about pressure.

Ordinarily, says Peter, people aren't going to harm you for

being enthusiastic for what is right. But sometimes they will. No matter what comes, he reminds us, none who are "valiant for truth" will miss their final reward. But here and now, Christians still have to deal with pressures. How do they face them? Just what do you do in a hostile environment?

Peter's first word of counsel has to do with *fear*. He looks back to a stormy era in the history of God's people, when fear almost engulfed them. When King Ahaz was told, " 'Syria is in league with Ephraim,' his heart and the heart of his people shook as the trees of the forest shake before the wind." In this situation came the word of the Lord through Isaiah: "Do not fear what they fear, nor be in dread. The Lord of hosts, him you shall regard as holy; let him be your fear and let him be your dread." At first, this sounds like cheap advice. Anyone can say, "Don't be afraid." But when others have the power to make you suffer, when your reputation is at stake or you may lose your job, it isn't an easy thing to rise above fear. Isaiah knew that and so did Peter. This word that comes from both prophet and apostle is not a superficial little pep talk. It offers a profound and practical alternative; namely, let the Lord Himself be the one whom you fear.

Keith Miller, in his book *The Second Touch*, calls this "playing it for God." He tells how a football player is delivered from over-much concern about crowd reaction when he plays for the eye of his coach, knowing that his every move will show up in the films on Monday morning. In like manner, Christians are delivered from fears of what others think when they "concentrate on being completely devoted to Christ in their hearts." Here again is one of Peter's favorite themes: The fear of the Lord puts other fears to flight.

Notice how naturally the apostle can substitute the word "Christ" here for Isaiah's "Lord of hosts." For Peter, to honor the God of Abraham, Isaac, and Jacob, and to reverence Christ as Lord is one and the same worship.

This displacement of fright by the fear of the Lord leads to freedom in witness. "Be ready at any time to give a quiet and reverent answer to any man who wants a reason for the hope that you have within you." Fear freezes our lips, numbs our testimony. Our failures to speak for Christ are more often due to timidity than to anything else. But when the overriding concern of our lives is to honor Christ, we become free to speak. So "be ready," says the apostle.

When your faith is challenged, when you are called on to give an account of what you believe, are you ready to answer? There is a sense in which we cannot and need not be formally prepared. Christ has promised that in such situations of trial we will be given what we are to say, and we need not be anxious about it beforehand. But that hardly excuses us from the obligation to know what we believe, and why. The Christian has good reasons for the hope that is in him, and he will be far more effective for Christ if he can present them. The fact that Christian faith cannot be arrived at by reason alone does not mean that it is not reasonable. But let your answer, when it is given, be "quiet and reverent." An overbearing attitude, a tone of superiority, will hardly commend the gospel. As someone has said, there is a difference between preaching the offense of the cross and preaching the cross offensively. Let's be sure that whatever reproach we bear is "the reproach of Christ"—not a reaction to our unpleasantness.

That brings us to a third instruction: "Make sure that your conscience is perfectly clean." When we are under heavy pressure, stunned by bitter and unfair attack, it is tempting to strike back. Sometimes our answer to the world's challenge may have something of personal venom in it. Peter cautions us against this. If we have knowingly wronged or offended others, our reasons for the hope within us can sound pretty hollow. The apostle Paul endeavored always to have a conscience void of offense toward God and man. Perhaps that was one secret of the power in his ministry. Labor, then, to be consistently Christian in every area of life—particularly in responding to the world's scorn. They may still, in Peter's words, "speak slanderously of you as rogues," but let your transparency of life give the lie to what they say. Peter has high hopes that through this holy strategy even the most violent of opposers may be won. "They may come to feel ashamed of themselves for libeling your good Christian behavior." In other words, let them say about your character what they will, but give them no grounds for their charges. Let your daily conduct prove them ridiculous. They may secretly wonder at what they revile. Hold steady, then, whatever they say. Your faithfulness when the pressure is on may be accomplishing more than you know.

Chapter Eighteen

the great introduction

*It is better to suffer for well-doing, if such should
be the will of God, than for doing wrong. For
Christ also died for our sins once and for all. He,
the just, suffered for the unjust, to bring us to God*
(I Peter 3:17-18, NEB).

Who can bring us moderns to the Eternal? Who can intro-
duce us to God?

To many of our contemporaries the question is prepos-
terous. For them, there is no God—no reality other than
man's experience of himself and his world. The cosmos has
no creator and history, no Lord. "God-language," we are
told, though it may refer to the depths of man's being or his
ultimate concern, cannot point to an eternal Thou whom he
can meet and know. When Paul Tillich, the famous theologian, was asked at Santa Barbara shortly before he died if he
ever prayed, he said, "No, but I meditate." Meditation, yes,
but no encounter, no drawing near, no relationship to a
personal God. Modern man is alone, we learn; and voices
directed Godward hear only their echo in response.

Many others, for whom the idea of God still makes sense,
find it quite unnecessary to be introduced to Him. What need
of formality here? Cannot every man approach Him when he
wishes? Find Him in your own way, we are advised, by "doing
your own thing." Since He is on the side of right, involve-
ment in any good cause will surely bring you to Him. The

modern paraphrase of an old text seems to run like this: "Find the Lord where you would like to seek him."

How vastly different is the outlook of the Bible! God can be known. Prophets and apostles all testify that we are made for Him. To meet Him, to dwell in His presence, to know and love Him—this is seen as the supreme goal of our life. This is the Bible's whole story. Long ago, at the dawn of our history, it was man with his Maker, in unclouded fellowship. And at the end, a great voice from the throne will say, "Behold the dwelling of God is with men. He will dwell with them and they shall be his people and God himself shall be with them." The Bible never argues for God's existence or His covenant. On every page it either assumes or affirms that God is real, and that He has created us to live with Him.

But we are living neither in the Garden of Eden nor in the New Jerusalem. Sadly, the Bible speaks also of banishment from the Garden, and of those who remain outside the gates of the city. Between Genesis 2 and Revelation 22 lies the record of our ruin and our redemption. It is the story of paradise lost and regained. But it is not man the hero who wins back what he has lost. No, right at the center of the history stands Jesus Christ, the God-Man. It is He, Peter says, who "died for our sins once and for all. He, the just, suffered for the unjust, to bring us to God."

Ever since sin broke the fellowship between man and God, God has been seeking to restore it. Reconciliation is His purpose and love is His name. First He chose a people for Himself. Though they were rebellious and wayward, He was pleased to dwell among them. Yet the very sign of His presence (the tabernacle and later the temple) bore also a reminder of the separation which sin had caused. The inner sanctuary—special place of God's presence—was shut off from all the people by a thick veil. None could enter there but the high priest, and he but once a year to offer sacrifices for the sins of the people. Thus the whole system of Jewish worship enshrined a twofold lesson: God seeks fellowship with men, but sin bars them from His presence.

Now, however, from Peter's perspective, the situation has been radically changed. Christ has "died for our sins." "Once for all"—with unrepeatable finality—He has removed the separating barrier between man and God. Matthew tells us that at Christ's death "the curtain of the temple was torn in two from top to bottom" (Matt. 27:51). By freely assuming responsibility for our guilt He exhausted its power to estrange us from God. A communion liturgy puts it vividly: "He cried out with a loud voice, 'My God, my God, why hast thou forsaken me' so that we might be accepted of God and never be forsaken of him." Here was the purpose of all that He did—that He might "bring us to God."

How does Peter happen to be teaching his fellow Christians about this? You will remember that he has been dwelling much on the problem of suffering in the life of the Christian community. He knows well (and so do most of them) that persecution and affliction lie ahead for them. But there are different kinds of suffering. Some is the natural outcome of our evils and blunders. It is a pity, says Peter, when a Christian has to suffer in this way—as an evildoer. But suffering "for righteousness' sake," suffering in a cause that is just and for a name that is revered—that is a different matter. When men and women suffer so, they follow in the steps of Christ. See how He, the just one, had to suffer!

As in I Peter 2:21-25, the apostle here is holding up Christ's death as an example. But the striking thing to note is that he cannot stop there. Once he fixes his attention on the cross, he cannot turn away without recalling its deeper meaning. There is something in Christ's passion which we can share, for we too may suffer unjustly. But at its heart is something we can never share, but can only receive with gratitude. For the sufferings of this "just one" were "for us, the unjust." The death He died was a death "for our sins." By standing in our place He has done for us what no other life or death could ever do: He has brought us to our Maker. He has ushered us into the presence of the Almighty. He has introduced us to God.

Have we felt the wonder of this? God is perfect love, but we are selfish and often hostile. He is just, but we have filled the world with our injustice. He is true, but even children can detect our phoniness. And yet because of Christ we may dwell with Him. We may call Him "Father." We may approach Him without the wretched burden of guilt and pretense. We may know His cleansing and the inflow of His strength. Best of all, we can begin to praise Him, to love Him, and to serve His will in this world. By His Spirit's power we can more and more be like Him and communicate His love to those around us. All this, because Christ has brought us to God.

We Christians pray, accordingly, "in Jesus' name"—not as a mere shibboleth, but because He is our mediator. We offer up our work and worship through Him, for He alone makes them acceptable. All our life with God roots in what our Lord has done, and continues to do for us.

Many, it is true, have never come to God, and doubt that they ever can. Others count it a trifling thing which they may handle in their own way. But Peter speaks for a grateful multitude who know that they know God, and who owe all they know to the suffering Savior.

Chapter Nineteen

"we're gonna win this game!"

In the body he was put to death; in the spirit he was brought to life. And in the spirit he went and made his proclamation to the imprisoned spirits. They had refused obedience long ago, while God waited patiently in the days of Noah and the building of the ark, and in the ark a few persons, eight in all, were brought to safety through the water. This water prefigured the water of baptism through which you are now brought to safety. Baptism is not the washing away of bodily pollution, but the appeal made to God by a good conscience; and it brings salvation through the resurrection of Jesus Christ, who entered heaven after receiving the submission of angelic authorities and powers, and is now at the right hand of God (I Peter 3:18-22, NEB).

We read in the past of the patriotic young Czech who tried to immolate himself in protest against the Russian occupation. His was the final gesture of despair. And it must be difficult *not* to despair when men see the liberties of a beloved homeland strangled by slow degrees before their eyes. What it was like for a Biafran as he saw his countrymen starving all around him, as he faced the dread possibility of genocide? How must life seem to the Arab refugees whose hopes for a secure dwelling place seem endlessly frustrated? And what must the future look like from inside a ghetto,

77

when the evils all around seem strong and malignant, and when possibilities of a better life seem mockingly small? It must be terribly hard to keep hoping, even when you're a Christian.

First century Christians found it hard, too. The powers arrayed against the infant church were formidable indeed. There was Rome with its awesome military might, poised to strike down any rival to Caesar. All around were deeply entrenched evils, seeming to defy all efforts toward redemptive change. But in the face of all this, those first believers showed remarkable calm and poise. We sense in their writings an almost incredible confidence. There is not a defeatist line in the New Testament.

Theirs was no naive optimism, either. You could hardly accuse them of holding rosy views about human nature. Nowhere is the ugliness of sin portrayed more realistically than in the recorded words of our Lord and His apostles. And what is more, they saw beyond this human lawlessness a dark kingdom of evil. They recognized a "prince of darkness" and "hosts of spiritual wickedness" behind the scenes. They beheld the entire creation "groaning in travail," the whole world "lying in the wicked one"; and yet they did not despair. What was their secret?

The early Christians rejoiced in hope because of the mighty things which God had done through His Son, Jesus Christ. Through His death on a cross, His resurrection, His ascension to the right hand of God, Christ had dealt decisively with the power of evil in this world. The apostle Peter has much to say about the suffering which Jesus bore, the harsh evil meted out to Him in this world. Reviled, rejected, murdered—the suffering Savior seemed no match for the foes arrayed against Him. "In the body he was put to death." But that was not the end of it. "In the spirit he was brought to life." The powers of death could not finally defeat Him.

Then, writes Peter, "He went and made his proclamation to the imprisoned spirits." Just who these imprisoned spirits were has been a puzzle to interpreters. We are told that they had "refused obedience long ago in the days of Noah." Some have felt that they represent human beings who perished in the Flood. But humans, dead or alive, are seldom referred to in Biblical literature as "spirits." It seems far more likely that these imprisoned spirits stand for the rebellious powers of evil that oppose God's gracious will. To these, Christ—the victor over death—made proclamation. The exact nature of this communication is not disclosed, but it must have been a heralding of victory.

The New Testament, as we have seen, uniformly presents Christ's cross and resurrection as the decisive defeat of Satan, the overthrow of his kingdom. God's purpose of love, in what seemed to be the moment of tragic defeat, won a great victory. Now Christ has entered heaven, having received "the submission of angelic authorities and powers." He is at the right hand of God. All authority is His in heaven and on earth. He has prevailed over all the dark forces that have held the creation in bondage. Christ is victor! Hallelujah!

This crucial triumph, however, does not mean that the warfare has ended. Sometimes wars drag on for many months, even when the final issue is no longer in doubt. Mopping-up operations continue. Pockets of resistance still hold out stubbornly, even though the ultimate victory has been assured. The victors may still lose a few skirmishes, but they have won the war.

But what role do Christians play in this cosmic conflict? Are they simply pawns in a vast struggle, spectators cheering from the sidelines? Or are they actively involved? Peter's words suggest the latter. In one sense God's redeemed ones are passive, the recipients of a mercy they did not merit and a redemption which they could not achieve. Just as God brought a few persons through the ordeal of the Flood and bore them to safety on the waters, so the church of Jesus Christ is preserved in the midst of a turbulent age through the waters of baptism. Not that the water itself has saving power. Peter hastens to add that "it brings salvation through the resurrection of Jesus Christ." In other words, it unites us to Him, the risen Lord. And this baptism, as Peter describes it, means more than an external washing. It is "the appeal made to God by a good conscience." In other words, baptism is not only an act of God, but also a pledge on the part of man. It is this idea which led to the application of the word *sacramentum,* or military oath, to baptism and the Lord's Supper. The Christian in baptism is confessing his faith in Christ, pledging his loyalty to Christ, committing himself to the service of Christ. Now, in this present age, he will toil, struggle, and suffer in conflict with the powers of evil. This is no sham struggle. He is really on the battle line. Yet he fights, even when against great odds, with triumphant confidence; for he knows the outcome of the struggle.

A high school basketball player, playing recently against highly touted opposition, encouraged his teammates at the end of each quarter with the assurance, "We're gonna win this game!" And win it they did. In their far more significant contest, Christians breathe the same confidence—not because of their skill and courage, but because they share in the great victory which Christ has already won. What room is there then for pessimism or whining in the ranks of the faithful? The causes we labor for may seem unpopular, and progress may be agonizingly slow, but none who serve the purpose of the risen Lord can ever finally fail. Never doubt it: "We're gonna win this game!"

Chapter Twenty

get your cross!

*Since therefore Christ suffered in the flesh, arm
yourselves with the same thought, for whoever has
suffered in the flesh has ceased from sin, so as to
live for the rest of the time in the flesh no longer
by human passions but by the will of God. Let the
time that is past suffice for doing what the Gentiles
like to do, living in licentiousness, passions, drunk-
enness, revels, carousing, and lawless idolatry. They
are surprised that you do not now join them in the
same wild profligacy, and they abuse you; but they
will give account to him who is ready to judge the
living and the dead. For this is why the gospel was
preached even to the dead, that though judged in
the flesh like men, they might live in the spirit like
God (I Peter 4:1-6, RSV).*

"God forbid, Lord! This shall never happen to you." Peter
was uncomfortable, even indignant. Who wants to hear about
suffering, rejection and death? He rebuked his Master for
speaking about a cross, and later balked at taking up his own.
But now, farther down the road, he feels quite differently.
He writes much now of Christ's dying—even seems to glory in
it. And in this passage, he calls all his fellow Christians to a
"dying life."

Here is the challenge: "Arm yourselves with the same
thought . . . " Remember Jesus setting His face to go to Jeru-

salem, resisting everything that would divert Him, choosing the path that led to the cross? Peter says that the same attitude must prevail in the lives of Christians. Let there be a moral decision to break with self-serving and self-saving. T. W. Manson paraphrases our Lord's call in these words: "Let him say No to himself, let him abjure his personal interests and be prepared, if need be, to accept a criminal's fate, if he wishes to follow me."

Cross bearing means having a fixed direction for the rest of your life. It is living, says Peter, "no longer by human passions." The behavior of most men is largely molded by their surroundings. David Riesman calls this life of conformity, "other direction." In his famous simile he likens the controls which mold contemporary character to "social radar," by which the individual sensitively notes the reactions of others to his behavior and modifies his course accordingly. Someone has captured the current philosophy in this mandate: "Find out what they're drinking and drink it, find out what they're thinking and think it, find out what they're wanting and want it." But when a man takes up his cross, none of these things determines his direction any longer. He walks by one standard—the will of God. He responds to one signal—"Lord, what will *you* have me to do?"

It is striking to note the motives which Peter introduces for this kind of life. The first is simply this: our Lord has borne *His* cross. "Since therefore Christ suffered in the flesh . . ." Peter is putting into his own words here the call of Christ, "If any man will come after me, let him deny himself, and take up his cross, and follow me." There is no real Christianity without this. And here the church needs to give a more certain sound. Somehow we have conveyed the impression that discipleship is an option for mature, spiritually advanced believers. The ordinary run-of-the-mill Christian, it is assumed, need not face such stern demands. But Christ has no such double standard. The call to salvation and the call to discipleship are one. Peter is saying, if you mean to be Christ's, then walk the way in which He walked—even when it means trouble.

The time past is more than enough for living the old way.

Note the touch of irony. "Let the time that is past suffice for doing what the Gentiles like to do." You've pampered yourself for a good while. You've tried that path. As you look back over it, Peter seems to imply, what did it get you? What real fulfillment did you find in it? Aren't you just a bit sick of it? These early Christians had a vivid sense of the crucial importance of time. Time is life; time is precious opportunity. Most of us have wasted far too much of it in living for ourselves. Enough of that!

What happens when you take this summons seriously? People "are surprised that you do not now join them in the same wild profligacy." To many around you, a life of cross-bearing seems strange madness. They scramble after the things which you renounce. They belittle causes for which you are ready to suffer. In their eyes, you are all wrong. Even when Christians suffer and die for their loyalty to God's will, many interpret this as a divine judgment! There were those, for example, who saw in Martin Luther King's death only a just condemnation: "He got what was coming to him." And there were some who said of the young missionaries martyred by the Aucas, "What a foolish waste of life and talent!" Yes, and those who conspired to murder Jesus thought that His death proved Him in the wrong. Christ and His followers are "judged in the flesh like men." But those who are so quick to judge them, says Peter, will themselves "give account to him who is ready to judge the living and the dead."

For those who follow Christ, the future gleams with hope. "The gospel was preached even to the dead" (that is, to those who die in Christ) for this purpose, "That though judged in the flesh like men, they might live in the spirit like God." Beyond death, they share God's life. True, suffering saints don't seem very impressive now. How must Jesus have looked when He walked toward Golgotha? A man with a cross on his back appears to be utterly defenseless. But it only seems that way. The cross is really his *armor.* "*Arm* yourselves with the same thought," says Peter. What appears to be a man's ruin is really his redemption. He throws his life away, but saves it in the process. The man who risks everything to do the will of God can never finally lose.

It may seem sheer madness to many, but this call to discipleship is the only rallying cry of genuine hope. After the death of Martin Luther King, strident voices were sounding in our streets, "Get your gun!" Sadly, for black or white, Jew or Arab, East or West, this way of life can only end in death. But after the dying and rising of Jesus Christ, Peter and a host of others can cry, "Get your cross." That is Christ's call, sounding once again in our time. May our generations hear it! His way of death leads to life.

Chapter Twenty-one

when the end is near

We are near the end of all things now, and you should therefore be calm, self-controlled men of prayer. Above everything else be sure that you have real deep love for one another, remembering how love can "cover a multitude of sins." Be hospitable to one another without secretly wishing you hadn't got to be! Serve one another with the particular gifts God has given each of you, as faithful dispensers of the magnificently varied grace of God. If any of you is a preacher then he should preach his message as from God. And in whatever way a man serves the Church he should do it recognizing the fact that God gives him his ability, so that God may be glorified in everything through Jesus Christ. To Him belong praise and power for ever, Amen! (I Peter 4:7-11, Phillips)

Thoughts about "the end of the world" have never made much sense to most Americans. Have you ever wondered why? Theologian Joseph Sittler suggests that the answer lies in the phenomenon of the American frontier. "When the historical experience of the whole people is interpreted in such a way as to affirm the *illimitable* by virtue of an open frontier existing for a long period of their history, then it surely follows that that declaration of the eschatological character of all existence will not easily address them with quick and intelligible meaning."[1] The frontier for Americans is more than a fact of national history. It has become a point of view, an outlook on life. And now, just as our westward expansion has ceased, we have found a new horizon for the illimitable—the space frontier. That makes it hard to think about a finale to everything, doesn't it? On the other hand, when people face absolute limits or boundaries, the thought of the end becomes very real to them.

But for the apostle Peter and the other New Testament writers, convictions about "the last things" had quite another source. The apostle's affirmation, "We are near the end of all things now," did not arise chiefly from the limiting character of life in the Roman Empire. He was not driven to think of a terminus to history merely as something inevitable. His conviction rested on the fact that history's great moment had already arrived. The kingdom of God had come with power in the life, death, and resurrection of Jesus Christ. The decisive victory of God's saving purpose for the world had been won. At any time now, the ascended Christ, the Lord of history, would be revealed in His glory. The early Christians lived in tiptoe anticipation of that appearing.

There are those in every age who make light of this expectation. "See how mistaken they were!" is the cry. "It's almost two thousand years later and still there is no sign of His coming." But wait a minute. It is remarkable to note that no New Testament writer ever predicted the time of Christ's return. They had learned from their Lord that no man knows the day or the hour. But they also learned from Him the importance of preparedness, the value of living in the light of the end—as though it was very near. This is what the apostle Peter is concerned about—not predicting when the end of all things will be, but urging his fellow Christians to come to terms here and now with the fact of the approaching end.

First, he wants them to have *cool heads*. Sometimes, teaching about the imminence of the end has served to unsettle the minds of people. In Thessalonica there were people who abandoned their daily tasks and gave way to

1. Joseph Sittler, *The Ecology of Faith*, p. 23.

frenzied excitement. In our own country, the Millerites once sold their homes and goods to prepare for what they supposed to be Christ's return on October 22, 1843. Peter, on the other hand, urges his hearers to "be calm, self-controlled men of prayer." Here he is paraphrasing the teaching of his Lord. Jesus had much to say about the importance of watchfulness and prayer while men await His coming. As history moves toward its conclusion, as the hearts of many are failing them for fear, and as the love of others is waxing cold, Christians are to be calm and steady in their faith, receiving through a disciplined prayer life (the word for "prayer" here is in the plural, pointing to a fixed habit of prayer) the strength they need to persevere.

Peter had learned from bitter experience how acute his own need was. At a time of grave testing he had been admonished by his Lord to pray, but had fallen asleep instead. His shameful denial and fall had etched indelibly on his mind the warning of his Master, "Watch and pray that you may not enter into temptation; the spirit indeed is willing, but the flesh is weak."

But living in the light of the end calls for more than cool heads. Peter wants *warm hearts.* "Above everything else, be sure that you have real deep love for one another." Too often, Christians have indulged in speculations about the future which were little more than curious. If mapping out "charts for the ages" leaves us hard and proud and critical, we have badly missed the way. A living hope in Christ's return doesn't keep us gazing at the heavens, but makes us alert to the needs of people around us. Note how Peter places this "above everything else." Just as Jesus called it His "new commandment," and as Paul insisted that we are "nothing" without it, so Peter wants to stress that love holds top priority.

What does he mean when he says that love can "cover a multitude of sins"? Surely not that by showing love to others we can cover up our own sins. All that Peter says about the atonement makes it plain that on that score Christ has done for us what we cannot do for ourselves. Actually, it is not our relationship with God which is principally in view here; Peter is talking about the covering of sin in our relationships with each other. Our love toward our brethren covers their sins with forgiveness. How much this is needed in the life of the church! All sorts of annoyances and problems arise in the church through our failures and foibles, and sometimes through our downright meanness. But where there is real love, these troubling evils within the church are neutralized, covered over, robbed of their power to divide and destroy.

One other practical manifestation of love which Peter mentions is hospitality. In the early days of the Christian church, when many believers were on the move and when worship was usually conducted in homes, the hospitality of God's people was sometimes strained to the breaking point. It is genuine love in action when we can welcome fellow Christians into our homes with an open heart, even when it is anything but convenient.

Peter now has a third charge for Christians who wait for their Lord. Cool of head and warm of heart, let them also have *ready hands*. "Serve one another with the particular gifts God has given each of you." This is a call to stewardship. Peter implies that no Christian is without his particular gifts and that each is to use them for the good of the church. How many of our Lord's parables strike this note! If you are expecting your Master to come back, the worst thing you can do is to be idle. Let everything that He has placed in your hands be invested in His service, always with an awesome sense of responsibility to Him. If your gift is speaking, then speak—as one who proclaims God's word and will, not your own. You are a messenger, not an improviser. And if your gift is some ministry of help to others, do it in dependence on God's strength. For the great goal of it all is not that your speaking or your service should be admired, but that "God may be glorified in everything through Jesus Christ." As you look forward, then, to the end of all things, nearer now than it has ever been before, let this high motivation guide all your life and service in the church; that through the prayerful, loving exercise of your every gift, the Lord of all may be abundantly praised. "To him belong glory and power forever, Amen!"

Chapter Twenty-two

suffering as a christian

Beloved, do not be surprised at the fiery ordeal which comes upon you to prove you, as though something strange were happening to you. But rejoice in so far as you share Christ's sufferings, that you may also rejoice and be glad when his glory is revealed. If you are reproached for the name of Christ, you are blessed, because the spirit of glory and of God rests upon you. But let none of you suffer as a murderer, or a thief, or a wrong-doer, or a mischief-maker; yet if one suffers as a Christian, let him not be ashamed, but under that name let him glorify God. For the time has come for judgment to begin with the household of God; and if it begins with us, what will be the end of those who do not obey the gospel of God? And "If the righteous man is scarcely saved, where will the impious and sinner appear?" Therefore let those who suffer according to God's will do right and entrust their souls to a faithful creator (I Peter 4:12-19, RSV).

"If one suffers as a Christian"—that's a big "if." Frankly, I wonder if many of us really have suffered that way. Oh, we've known something of illness in our families, of grief and pain. But almost everyone goes through those things sooner or later. Some of us have made bad blunders and gotten into serious trouble because of them; but there's nothing uniquely

Christian about that, is there? Peter says, "If one suffers *as a Christian*." That's different. That comes to you because you are identified with Jesus Christ. Perhaps it's because you speak of Him and His truth to people who don't want to hear it. Or you stand for His will among many who don't care to do it. Or maybe you just let your light shine around those who prefer to live in the twilight zone. And so they give you a hard time.

Do you ever ask yourself, "Why doesn't this happen to me?" For most of us, the answer to that one is not very difficult. The unbelieving world doesn't resent our witness because we don't often speak about Christ. We pride ourselves a bit on not being high-pressure, hard-sell evangelists. We're almost too reserved and polite ever to bother anyone with the claims of Jesus Christ. And then, most of us are not upsetting people by what we do, either. We don't cause any disturbances. We don't threaten any entrenched interests. We don't throw ourselves into controversial causes. No, we leave that to the hippies and the student radicals and a few wild-eyed "liberal" preachers. We mind our own business, and who's going to get mad at us for doing that? To be brutally honest about it, most of us don't suffer as Christians, because there isn't very much that's distinctively Christian about us. You might say that we've sold our spiritual birthright for a mess of middle-class morality. Since the real thing might get us into hot water, we manage somehow to play it cool.

The first century Christians hadn't learned this art, apparently. They were not very clever or skillful at hiding their true identity. People around them knew who and what they were, and often found them highly disturbing. So Peter had to warn them, "Watch out, you Christians; there's trouble ahead." "Beloved, do not be surprised at the fiery ordeal which comes upon you." If anyone seriously tries to serve Jesus Christ and to see His will done in this world, he shouldn't be shocked at the fireworks that may follow. Just think back to the way Christ was treated. That should take all the surprise out of it. The Christian who carries on his Master's program can expect his Master's welcome—a warm welcome with some and a very hot one with others. He's going to "share Christ's sufferings."

Maybe I've misjudged you. Maybe you're going through something very much like this right now. Then, says Peter, rejoice. Be glad, because to be identified now with the suffering Savior means to share in the coming joy when He is revealed in His glory. In case that call to rejoicing sounds like a piece of dreamy, impossible advice, remember who was writing it. Peter had been able to try this out himself. He and John had been beaten until their backs were crisscrossed with livid welts, but they went home "rejoicing that they were counted worthy to suffer dishonor for the Name." They had experienced a kind of miracle in undergoing all that.

I remember hearing a Latvian Christian tell about what it was like to face a Russian firing squad because of his testimony to Jesus Christ. Having narrowly escaped, he told of the indescribable sense of God's presence and power with him in the hour of testing. He found, as Peter did, that there is blessing in reproach that is borne for Christ's sake, "because the spirit of glory and of God rests upon you." That's why you can rejoice: He is with you.

So don't be "ashamed" when the reproach comes, continues Peter. Some will try to make you ashamed. They will brand you as an enemy of the human race. They will find ways to malign your motives and ridicule what you do. They will despise you. Maybe they'll call you a "fanatic" or a "fundamentalist" or a "nigger-lover," depending on whose skin you are getting under at the time. But don't be ashamed. Don't worry about the names they call you. Concentrate on the name that God has given you: Christian. Instead of being ashamed of it, so live up to it that God will be praised.

But even when we do suffer as Christians, we can't afford the luxury of a martyr complex. At our best we are far from innocent sufferers. It is never a clearcut case of the "good guys" against the "bad guys." *God* has a hand in these afflictions, and they are meant to accomplish something in us. Peter has already said that the ordeal comes "to prove you." Now he calls it a divine judgment. "For the time has come for judgment to begin with the household of God." This has always been a hard thing for the covenant people to accept. What? The chosen people—the apple of God's eye—in line for judgment? It seemed impossible, but it happened. It happened to Israel time and again. And it happens to the church. Jesus is the promised Lord who "suddenly comes to his temple." His first work is to "purify the sons of Levi and refine them like gold and silver." Even God's beloved children feel His chastening rod, His purging fire. If this is so, reasons Peter, what must it be like for those who disobey the gospel? If the Lord's people must pass through such severe trials, what awful woes must await the ungodly?

When you suffer as a Christian, therefore, receive it as from God's hand. Beware of the discouragement that would tempt you to go back on your discipleship. Don't let persecution make you bitter or goad you into what you know is wrong. Rather, says Peter, in the face of the worst kind of wrongs, continue to "do right." With your eyes in faith on the one who prayed, "Father, forgive them" and "Into thy hands I commit my spirit," go on forgiving and commit your soul to the same Father. Peter seems to predict here for others what he later experienced himself: suffering "as a Christian" may go all the way to the offering up of one's life. But it is no leap into the void. Waiting to receive you, says Peter, is "a faithful creator."

Chapter Twenty-three

attention, church leaders

*And now I appeal to the elders of your commu-
nity, as a fellow-elder and a witness of Christ's
sufferings, and also a partaker in the splendour that
is to be revealed. Tend that flock of God whose
shepherds you are, and do it, not under compulsion, but of your own free will, as God would have
it; not for gain but out of sheer devotion; not
tyrannizing over those who are allotted to your
care, but setting an example to the flock. And
then, when the Head Shepherd appears, you will
receive for your own the unfading garland of
glory"* (I Peter 5:1-4, NEB).

You leaders in the church of Jesus Christ, this message is
especially for you. Peter is addressing "elders," but by that
term he means all who have any part in the "care of souls." If
you are a minister or a ruling elder in your congregation, if
you teach a Sunday school class or direct a young people's
group, if you counsel and encourage your fellow Christians,
or if you are simply a parent seeking to nurture your children
in the faith, here is your commissioning.

Notice first Peter's approach. He writes as a "fellow-elder,"
one identified with us, sharing in our task. He shares our
hope, too, as "a partaker in the splendour that is to be
revealed." But also (and herein lies his special authority) he
writes as "a witness of Christ's sufferings." This was the
hallmark of apostleship: to have been an eyewitness of the
events surrounding Christ's death and resurrection.

When read in the light of the apostle's own experience, this whole passage has a remarkable poignancy about it. "Tend that flock of God whose shepherds you are." This had been his Master's personal charge to him. "Simon, son of John, do you love me? . . . Tend my sheep." It was the word which shamed and exalted him, which reinstated him and gave him his task. Now he passes it on to his brethren. The word "tend" includes the whole of the shepherd's care for his flock. It means provision, guidance, and watchful oversight.

But the apostle assumes here that these leaders know what their pastoral duties are. He is mainly concerned about the way in which they go about them. He offers three sets of guidelines, each containing a negative and a positive—one pattern to be followed, another to be shunned. The first is this: "not under compulsion but of your own free will, as God would have it." Peter is raising the question of our motive for ministry. Why do we carry on a ministry of shepherding? Why call on people, why watch for their souls? Because we have to? Because it is expected of us? Why do we accept the position of elder or teacher? Because no one else was willing to be considered? Service of that kind is better than none. But Peter points out a better way: "willingly, as God would have it." The Greek means literally "according to God," which can mean either "in a godly way" or "for God's sake." In either case the impulse for our ministry is to grow out of our relationship to the God of grace. True shepherds labor not as grumbling hired servants, but as willing sons.

The second couplet probes more deeply into our motivation: "not for gain but out of sheer devotion." What are we really after in our care of souls? One possibility is never far from any of us. We may do it "for shameful gain." Few, perhaps, would be so crass as to carry on their work solely for money, although financial considerations may sometimes weigh more heavily than anything else in decisions about a minister's place of service. But there are motives for gain which are more refined, though no less shameful. A pastor can visit his people with an eye to the large number of calls he can report to his consistory. He can preach with a passion for people's praise. Peter knew that peril as well as any man and urges us instead to serve "out of sheer devotion." Let a man minister with eagerness because he loves people. Let those who lead God's church so care for those they shepherd that they will "very gladly spend and be spent for them," without any thought of personal reward. It makes a great deal of difference whether a man has the spirit of a hireling or the heart of a shepherd.

The apostle's last charge deals with actual practice—how we wear the mantle of leadership: "not tyrannizing over those who are allotted to your care, but setting an example to the flock." They are "allotted to your care"; that is, they are the Lord's people and He has entrusted them to you. He has made you responsible for them. Therefore, says the apostle, never treat them as though they were your slaves or subjects. Never govern them with harshness or self-will. Never despise them or assume that they are beneath you. Lead them, rather, by way of example. This doesn't mean, of course, that the minister or elder is a professional holy man whom all others must imitate. But it does mean that Christian leadership without Christian living is an impossibility. True, your role is more that of a coach than of a star player. But why not aim at being a combination player-coach? Don't just tell them—*show* them.

Now, after this call to selfless motivation and exemplary living comes the promise: "When the head shepherd appears, you will receive for your own the unfading garland of glory." How richly strange are God's ways! Those who serve for love's sake, without thought of reward, are those whom He rewards. This is "grace upon grace." It is unspeakably wonderful simply to belong to Jesus Christ, to receive forgiveness and new life through Him. It is an incomparable added privilege to serve His church and care for His people. To think, then, that when the chief Pastor appears, there could be a "garland of glory" for those already so blessed is almost overwhelming. Here, if anywhere, we meet "amazing grace." Lord, grant us a fitting gratitude!

Chapter Twenty-four

the well-dressed christian

You younger members must also submit to the elders. Indeed all of you should defer to one another and wear the "overall" of humility in serving each other. God is always against the proud, but he is always ready to give grace to the humble. So, humble yourselves under God's strong hand, and in his own good time he will lift you up. You can throw the whole weight of your anxieties upon him, for you are his personal concern (I Peter 5:5-7, Phillips).

"Wear the 'overall' of humility." Here is standard dress for the Christian. In all seasons, on every occasion, this rather plain-sounding garb is in good taste. It was the uniform which our Lord habitually wore.

In fact, Peter's language here (comparing humility to a garment) probably was inspired by what he saw at the Last Supper. Remember John's record of it? "Jesus, knowing that the Father had given all things into his hand and that he had come from God and was going to God, rose from supper, laid aside his garments and girded himself with a towel. Then he poured water into a basin and began to wash the disciples' feet and to wipe them with the towel with which he was girded" (John 13:3-5). Peter remembered that well. How could he forget it? He had protested indignantly and had learned a humbling lesson. Now he calls his brethren to learn it, too. Let them lay aside the trappings of pride and gird themselves in humility to serve each other.

The example of Christ is reason enough for self-humbling. But there are other powerful incentives as well. "God is always against the proud." Peter is quoting a proverb here which, like many other passages of Scripture, shows God's special resistance to human pride. Of all the evils which the Lord hates, "haughty eyes" head the list (Prov. 6:16,17). Peter uses a military term here to describe the divine opposition. God "sets himself," or "deploys his forces," against the proud. It is a signal part of His government of the world that He seeks out the proud man to bring him low. Perhaps it is because pride is the essence of rebellion against God. It is man's effort to replace Him, to usurp His throne. By asserting himself, a proud man seeks to be higher than the Most High and thus is put down. On the other hand, God is "always ready to give grace to the humble." Those who are lowly He lifts; those who are empty He fills; to those who know their need of Him He is unspeakably rich in mercy.

Most of us, in theory, at least, have no quarrel with this procedure. We agree that the proud should be leveled and the humble exalted. In fact, we view the fall of those whom we deem proud with considerable glee. Our problem is that we can much more easily identify pride in others than we can in ourselves. And we are far too ready to imagine that we are the humble ones upon whom God smiles! But what does it mean to be humble? How do you humble yourself? How does this beautiful principle work itself out in everyday life?

Peter has some very practical suggestions. "You younger members must also submit to the elders." The apostle, we remember, has just instructed the elders of the flock that they are to rule not as tyrants but as winsome examples. Now he speaks to those who are younger. Whether we are children in the home, students in a school, or members of a flock, we show humility by submission to our elders—respect and deference to those who are older than we and who are entrusted with responsibility for us. Now, admittedly, the young often excel their elders in gifts and intelligence. It is sheer folly to ignore the contribution they can make. But is it not an unbecoming arrogance for them to assume that they are wiser and better than many who are riper in experience?

"When I was fourteen," said a young man, "my dad didn't know anything. But when I was twenty-one," he continued, "I was amazed at how much the old boy had learned in seven years!"

But humility is not a grace which only the young need to cultivate. Peter says, "Indeed, all of you should defer to one another." If it is pride in a young person to withhold respect from his elders, it is just as unlovely for the old to insist stiffly that every younger person should submit to them. The questions we all need to grapple with are these: How ready are we to listen to each other, to respect one another's opinions? How careful are we to deal with one another as persons, each sensitive to the feelings of others? How ready are we to serve in unassuming ways? How much of the "towel and basin" ministry are we actually practicing?

This horizontal dimension to humility is a vital one. Any claims to humility are patently false if we are unbending and inconsiderate in our relationships with others. But there is a vertical dimension, too. "Humble yourselves under God's strong hand." How, we might ask, does a person do that? "God's strong hand" here refers to His providential dealing in our lives. How do we react to the circumstances in which we are placed, to our lot in life? Some circumstances, of course, we can change and ought to change. But there are many factors that bear upon our lives over which we have little control. How do we react to these? Grumbling and murmuring about our portion in life is a sure mark of pride. To fret and chafe against God's appointments is to find fault with Him. Why did He not give us better opportunities? Some other partner for our life? Some more congenial occupation? Beneath such questions is a wounded pride and self-will. We feel that we deserve better treatment from God and consider ourselves unfairly used. To humble ourselves under His hand, however, is to acknowledge the wisdom and love behind His ways with us. Peter assures us that if we cheerfully accept His will for our lives, He—in His own good time—will lift us up.

This is easy to talk about, but not so easy to apply. Sometimes our ways are anything but pleasantness and peace.

We see little evidence of God's hand in our affairs and we tremble with anxiety about what may be ahead. How good to know that we can throw the whole weight of our anxieties on Him! If we humbly submit to His leading and teaching, we can roll the whole weight of our concern on Him with confidence. For, says Peter, "you are his personal concern."

The connection of this last promise with what has gone before is not immediately apparent. What does it have to do with humility? Actually, the connection is very close. We are tempted to be proud because we desperately want to feel important. We need to feel that we matter, that we are "somebody." The most liberating thing in the world is to realize in the light of the gospel that we do matter, that we are important to God. Then we can stop our feverish scrambling to be somebody "on our own." It seems strange to say, but there is nothing so deeply humbling as to know that we are greatly loved.

Chapter Twenty-five

how to be a rock

*Be sober, be watchful. Your. adversary the devil
prowls around like a roaring lion, seeking some one
to devour. Resist him, firm in your faith, knowing
that the same experience of suffering is required of
your brotherhood throughout the world. And after
you have suffered a little while, the God of grace,
who has called you to his eternal glory in Christ,
will himself restore, establish, and strengthen you.
To him be the dominion for ever and ever. Amen* (I
Peter 5:8-11, RSV).

How does a man of sand become a rock? The great apostle
could write about that with firsthand conviction. "You are
Simon, son of John," Jesus had said. "You shall be called
Cephas (that is, Peter, the Rock)" (John 1:42, NEB). Now
Peter dips his pen, as it were, in his own blood and writes out
of the shame and triumph of his personal experience. What
did it take to be a rock?

First of all, it took a sober warning. "Simon, Simon,
behold Satan demanded to have you that he might sift you
like wheat" (Luke 22:31). Do you hear the echo of this in
Peter's admonition to his brethren? "Your adversary the devil
prowls around like a roaring lion, seeking some one to
devour." No man will be Gibraltar-like in the Christian conflict who doesn't know what he is up against. Awareness of
the enemy is essential for victory. Just how successful could
our armed forces be in battle if they lacked all knowledge of
the foe? Or worse, if they imagined that he did not exist?

The devil uses many strategies to gain his ends. At some times and in some places he goes underground. In other ages he boldly intimidates his victims. At one time people saw goblins in bushes, fiends in forests, and witches in harmless women. Then, for a time, he kept in circulation the rumor that he was a myth. He masqueraded as a medieval superstition, a ridiculous fellow with horns and hoofs, or a theme for crude jokes. Now he is taking full advantage of the avid interest in the occult, and Satan worship is practiced even among educated people in our land.

Christ knew of the malignant, personal power of Satan. Nor were Christ's followers unaware of his fearful power. An outstanding Biblical scholar has recently pointed out that the New Testament evidence for the existence and personality of the devil is of the same order as that for the existence and personality of God. Our Lord knew what it was to contend with the devil—to be almost overwhelmed in His last hours by the power of darkness. And He knew what subtle perils lay ahead for His followers.

Still today, our enemy the devil is "always about." Sometimes, serpentlike, he charms and beguiles us, making the way of evil seem seductively desirable. Or again, he comes as an angel of light with gilded half-truths, quoting Scripture for his purpose. Or sometimes, as in Peter's day, he is a "roaring lion," rending Christ's flock with the fangs of persecution or under the claws of slander and abuse. Make no mistake of it, Christian, he is a destroyer. He would have us abandon our faith and deny our Master. He seeks our final ruin.

"Be sober, be watchful," says Peter. Is he hearing another voice as he writes? "Simon, are you asleep? Could you not watch one hour? Watch and pray that you may not enter into temptation" (Mark 14:37-38). Yes, stay alert. Keep your wits about you. Be on guard against every onslaught of temptation, for only the vigilant can hope to stand. Whatever dulls the faculties and numbs the conscience, whatever so engrosses us as to make Christ and His lordship seem unreal, plays right into the tempter's hands.

Reconnaissance alone, however, has never won a war. Peter calls for more than that. "Resist him, firm in your faith."

Note that: "resist him." There is not a word in the Bible that counsels us to flee from the devil. Paul, it is true, tells us to "flee youthful lusts." There are times when, as Joseph fled from Potiphar's wife, we need to run from compromising circumstances. But Christians are to resist the devil. They are to "stand up to him." How is this done? For the believers of Peter's day, it meant refusing to be intimidated by the lion's roar, refusing to flinch or curb their testimony under persecution. It meant steadfastly doing right while they suffered one wrong after another from a pagan society. Someone has suggested that we can resist the devil most effectively when we cultivate virtues opposite to the sins he suggests. When tempted to a cowardly silence, we speak out the more boldly. When pressured to fight fire with fire, we return good for evil. If the devil's whisper seeks to make us proud, we go out of our way to serve in meekness.

But the greatest resource for resistance lies in our faith itself. Resist the devil "firm in your faith." That word "firm" speaks of an extreme hardness, a flintlike resolution. Stand immovable in your faith, trusting in Jesus Christ, relying on His Spirit's power within you. Refuse to give an inch. Hold fast to the sword of God's Word and make it your weapon. Remember the battle plan of Jesus in the wilderness? "It is written . . . it is written . . . it is written." Through the whole armor that God provides you, hold your own with an unyielding faith.

Peter now mentions another incentive to this steadfastness. "The same experience of suffering is required of your brotherhood throughout the world." Let Christians remember that they never fight alone. They are members of one body. When one member suffers, the others suffer with it. Struggles and trials are family matters for God's people. That thought can put fresh heart in us. In one sense, it is small comfort to be told in our misery that others are worse off than we. But when we fight at some lonely outpost against seemingly great odds, it is good to know that we are part of a fellowship, united in a common cause. The defensive lineman on the football field hits harder and with more confidence when he knows that the teammates on either side of him are also "giving 100 percent." And how many soldiers at the front have found undreamed-of courage when they witnessed the selfless heroism of their buddies?

Well, is that all we need to be men of rock? A warning and a challenge? If we watch and struggle together, is that enough? No, Peter knew it took more than that. There was also the promise of a faithful Lord. "I have prayed for you that your faith may not fail . . . . Now I tell you that you are Peter the rock, and it is on this rock that I am going to found my church and the powers of death will never prevail against it" (Luke 22:32; Matt. 16:18, Phillips).

The Lord who called him had promised to make him stand. How like the assurance which Peter now gives to the church! "The God of all grace, who has called you to his eternal glory in Christ, will himself restore, establish, and strengthen you." Their struggle will not be easy or pleasant, but it will be "for a little while." After stern testings, after bitter anguish, sometimes after their own shameful stumbling, the Lord will restore His people. He will establish them, He will strengthen them. In other words, He will build His church. Here is our confidence. We watch, we pray, we fight; but in the deepest sense "the battle is the Lord's." In all our efforts to build the church, the real work is His. And He will perfect it. He will make us what we are meant to be.

How to be a rock? Here is Peter's own charge: "So come to him, our living Stone—the stone rejected by men but choice and precious in the sight of God. Come, and let yourselves be built as living stones into a spiritual temple" (2:4, 5, NEB). Men of sand who trust in Christ are destined to be rocklike. They will never be moved. "To him be the dominion for ever and ever. Amen."